Peacemaking
Responding to Conflict Biblically

Facilitator's Guide

By: Ken Sande
Small group format by Dr. Jimmy Ray Lee and Brad Rymer

Communications should be addressed to:
Turning Point Ministries, Inc.   **or**   Peacemaker® Ministries
P. O. Box 22127   1537 Avenue D, Suite 352
Chattanooga, TN 37422-2127   Billings, MT 59102
Email: info@turningpointministries.org   Email: mail@HisPeace.org

ISBN 1-58119-044-1

Layout: Louise Lee

Web-sites

Peacemaker® Ministries

www.HisPeace.org

Turning Point Ministries

www.TurningPointMinistries.org

About the Author

Ken Sande is the founder and president of Peacemaker® Ministries. He is an engineer and attorney who has used biblical peacemaking principles since 1982 to help resolve thousands of conflicts, including business, employment, and family disputes; church divisions; and complex lawsuits. He is a member of the national panel of arbitrators of the American Arbitration Association and has served on the board of directors of the Christian Legal Society and the Dispute Resolution Committee of the State Bar of Montana. He presently serves on the board of directors of the Christian Counseling and Educational Foundation in Philadelphia, Pennsylvania. Ken is a Certified Christian Conciliator™ and is the author of numerous resources on conflict resolution, including *The Peacemaker: A Biblical Guide to Resolving Personal Conflict.*

About the Small Group Editors

Dr. Jimmy Ray Lee is founder and president of Turning Point Ministries, Inc. He has authored *Understanding the Times* and numerous small group studies published by Turning Point. Under the direction and guidance of Dr. Lee, Turning Point produced *Living Free*—a high-impact, video-based training. This training helps churches develop Christ-centered small groups that deal with the contemporary problems people face today.

Dr. Lee is the founder and honorary chairman of Project 714 (now known as STARS), a chemical prevention/intervention program for schools. He also founded Ark Ministries, an inner-city ministry that reached 600 to 700 young people weekly. He started the Chattanooga Teen Challenge and served as president for three years. Jimmy was executive director of the Nashville Teen Challenge during its formative years.

Jimmy has served as pastor, area youth director, and hospital chaplain. He has earned a master of divinity and doctor of ministry from Luther Rice Seminary. In 1983, he was awarded the "Service to Mankind Award" presented by the Highland Sertoma Club in Hixson, Tennessee.

Brad Rymer is actively involved in leading Turning Point groups and serves on the Turning Point Board of Directors. He and his wife, Babs, co-chaired the *Living Free* video project.

Trained in conflict mediation at the Institute for Christian Conciliation (a division of Peacemaker® Ministries), Brad is a Tennessee Supreme Court Rule 31 Mediator, Christian Conciliator and Conflict Counselor. He is a member of the Academy of Family Mediators and Mediation Association of Tennessee.

Brad coordinated this small group project with Peacemaker® Ministries and Turning Point Ministries. He serves on the board of directors with the Chattanooga Resource Foundation and First Things First.

Peacemaking
Responding to Conflict Biblically

Contents

Facilitator's Guide: *Peacemaking*, Turning Point, P. O. Box 22127, Chattanooga, TN 37422-2127

Preface

Peacemaker® Ministries and Turning Point Ministries have joined together to produce this small group curriculum—*Peacemaking: Responding to Conflict Biblically*. This small group bible study is based on *The Peacemaker* (second edition) by Ken Sande.

The approach used in *Peacemaking* to resolving conflict may be summarized in four basic principles:

Glorify God (1 Corinthians 10:31). Biblical peacemaking is motivated and directed by a desire to please and honor God. His interests, reputation, and commands should take precedence over all other considerations. This focus not only shows our love and respect for God but also protects us from the impulsive, self-centered decisions that make conflicts even worse.

Get the log out of your eye (Matthew 7:5). Peacemaking requires facing up to our own attitudes, faults, and responsibilities before pointing out what others have done wrong. Overlooking the minor offenses of others and honestly admitting our own faults often will encourage similar responses from our opponents and open the way for candid dialogue, reconciliation, and constructive negotiation.

Go and show your brother his fault (Matthew 18:15). At times, peacemaking also requires constructive confrontation. When others fail to accept responsibility for their actions, we may need to confront them in a gracious yet firm manner. If they refuse to respond appropriately, we may need to involve respected friends, church leaders, or other neutral individuals who can help restore peace.

Go and be reconciled (Matthew 5:24). Finally, peacemaking involves a commitment to restoring damaged relationships and developing agreements that are just and satisfactory to everyone involved. Forgiveness and cooperative negotiation clear away the debris left by conflict and make possible reconciliation and genuine peace.

This course shows how these principles may be applied in the home, workplace, church, and neighborhood. Among other things it explains:

- How to use conflict as an opportunity to please and honor God.

- Why Christians should resolve disputes in church and not in court.

- Why you can trust God to help you even in the most difficult conflicts.

- When it is appropriate simply to overlook an offense.

- When it is appropriate to confront others regarding sinful behavior.

As you learn to deal with these issues in a biblical way, you can develop an entirely new approach to resolving conflict. Instead of reacting to disputes in a confused, defensive, or angry manner, you can learn to manage conflict confidently and constructively. This material describes the principles required for effective conflict management. This study is designed for small group interaction and can be used in home groups, support groups, cell groups, and Sunday school. The material is also applicable for personal study. May the Lord bless, challenge, and encourage you in this study.

Getting Started

Group Size

We suggest that each *Peacemaking* group have two group leaders (facilitators) and a maximum of 12 participants. Having more than 12 may prevent some from being a part of much-needed discussion.

Preparation Time

The facilitator's material is written in an almost word-for-word dialogue. However, it is hoped that as you come to know and understand the concepts presented, you will be able to "personalize" each session to better fit your own style. Highlight the points you want to emphasize and make notes for yourself. Also, for further study for each session, we recommend the book entitled *The Peacemaker* by Ken Sande.

Your group is unique—so adapt questions to their needs and situations. Be sensitive to each person who is in your group.

Keep in mind that the answers provided for the discussion questions are there only as a tool to assist you and may not be the only "right" answers to the questions being asked.

Become thoroughly familiar with the four elements of each session:
- Introduction
- Self-Awareness
- Spiritual Awareness
- Application

You will find more detail about these on the following page.

The facilitators should meet prior to each session to pray and make final plans. They should also meet briefly after each session to discuss what happened during the meeting and go over any follow-up that may be needed.

***Peacemaking* Group Member Guides**

Before Session 1, the *Peacemaking* group member guides should be distributed to each group member. Facilitators should be thoroughly familiar with the material before the first meeting.

During the *Orientation*, you will encourage group members to complete the appropriate assignments prior to each group meeting. Through the readings and other exercises in the group member guide, group members can come to each session better prepared for meaningful discussion.

Correlation Between Facilitator's Guide and Group Member Guide

Facilitator's Guide — This guide is designed to lead the group through the four-phase small group format. The facilitator's responsibility is to start the discussion, give it direction, and thereafter simply keep the discussion personal and on track.

The text is presented in the left column. The right column contains tips and pointers for leading the group along with answers to questions. The facilitator will prayerfully present select questions because there are usually more questions than time permits.

Although the text is presented in the Group Member's Guide,

it may not in some cases be word for word as in the Facilitator's Guide. For example, the Introductions are different in the two guides. The Facilitator's Guide is directed toward opening prayer and go-around question; whereas, the Group Member's Guide focuses on devotions for the week which is a part of preparation for the upcoming session.

Group Member's Guide — This guide is designed to be done as homework preparing the participant for meaningful ministry during the small group session. Although the general text is the same as Self-Awareness, Spiritual Awareness, and Application in the Facilitator's Guide, concentration should be on the group process during the actual group experience.

It is good for the participant to bring the Group Member's Guide to the group session; however, the participant should be more attentive to the group process rather than trying to find text or written answers in the Group Member's Guide. Each group member should bring a Bible for meaningful study and application of God's Word for daily living.

In a Nutshell — The Facilitator's Guide is designed to lead the group process through *Peacemaking*. The Group Member's Guide will prepare the participant for the group meeting.

Facilitator's Guide: *Peacemaking*, Turning Point, P. O. Box 22127, Chattanooga, TN 37422-2127

Suggested Group Format

The group format for each session consists of four elements: Introduction, Self-Awareness, Spiritual Awareness, and Application. There is a reason for each phase. The facilitators should always plan each session with this format in mind.

Part I Introduction
(10 minutes)

Begin with prayer. The facilitator may pray or may ask one of the group members to lead in prayer. After the prayer, a sharing question helps put the group at ease and makes the members more comfortable in being a part of the discussion. The lead facilitator should respond to the sharing question first, followed by the co-facilitator. This helps the group members to feel safer in participating in the exercise. After the facilitators have shared, the group members will share one after another around the circle. Always remind group members they are not expected to share if they do not wish to do so. The rule is that everyone works within his or her comfort level and is welcome to pass.

This is not the time for detailed conversation, so ask the members of the group to keep their comments brief. If a person is obviously in pain during the exercise, the facilitator should interrupt the sharing and pray for the person in pain. After prayer, the exercise may resume.

Part II Self-Awareness
(20-25 minutes)

After the sharing question, the facilitator will lead the group into the Self-Awareness phase. Self-Awareness is a time to discuss the practical issues involved in *Peacemaking*. It is important to stay on the subject matter. This is a time to focus on needs and healing, not to have a "martyr" or "pity party."

It is suggested in Self-Awareness that the facilitators ask the group members to share as they wish rather than going around the circle as in the Introduction phase. This is because people are at various comfort levels, and they should not feel pressured to self-disclose if they are uncomfortable. As the group continues to meet, members will feel more and more comfortable in being a part of the discussion.

Remember, prayer is always in order. If a group member is hurting during this phase, stop and pray. One of the facilitators may lead in prayer or ask another group member to pray. This says to the group members that each one is important and that you care about each individual.

Part III Spiritual Awareness
(20-25 minutes)

After the Self-Awareness phase, the facilitator will lead the group into the bible study time. Having briefly explained the topic, the facilitator should assign Scriptures listed in the Facilitator's Guide to group members. When each Scripture is called by the facilitator, the group member should read the verse(s). After the verses are read, give time for discussion.

Part IV Application
(20 minutes)

This part is actually a continuation of Part III. Ask for volunteers to share their reflections on the question. The facilitators should emphasize the importance of the group members' applying biblical principles to their lives. Help begins with right thinking. The Bible says, "Be transformed by the renewing of your mind" (Romans 12:2). Obedience to the Word should follow with right behavior. Right feelings will follow right thinking and right behavior.

Orientation

Introduction

Allow 10 Minutes

Opening Prayer

> Thank God for each person who has taken the step of choosing to join the *Peacemaking* group. Pray for the Holy Spirit's guidance on all that takes place in your group.

Sharing Question

Welcome to the *Peacemaking* group. I would like to begin this first session by having each of us in the group introduce him/herself and tell why you were drawn to this group. I will start by telling you that my name is _____.

> The purpose of this exercise is to help group members move toward being more comfortable in sharing with the group. Ask each one to introduce him/herself, beginning with yourself and your co-facilitator.

Self-Awareness

Allow 20–25 Minutes

We are glad for each of you who has joined this group. By way of introduction, I want to spend a few minutes talking about the purpose of this group and what our procedures will be each week.

> Read pages 9-15 and 235-237 from *The Peacemaker* for further preparation for this session.

The *Peacemaking* group is a small group (usually fewer than 12 people) who want to better understand issues of conflict in a biblical way which can be an entirely new approach to resolving conflict. Instead of reacting to disputes in a confused, defensive, or angry manner, we can learn to **respond to conflict** confidently and constructively.

In this group we will look at the principles required for effective conflict management and provide numerous illustrations of how they have been used to resolve actual disputes and lawsuits. (The stories told in the *Peacemaking* material are based on real situations, but the names of the people and distinguishing facts have been changed to protect the privacy of those involved.)

Here are the elements of a typical meeting.

Meeting Format

Introduction: First we will pray together. Prayer is always appropriate during our meetings, especially as we begin our time together. After we begin with prayer, we will then spend a few minutes talking and getting to know each other better. We hope this will grow to be a group of caring and supportive friends, but in any of our conversations here, you should never feel pressured to talk. We only want you to speak when you feel comfortable speaking.

Self-Awareness: Next in our meeting comes something we call our "Self-Awareness" time. This part of our meeting is designed to help us take a look at our life and better understand the pitfalls and delusion we often face. During Self-Awareness (about 20 minutes), we will discuss some of the practical issues involved in understanding and dealing with conflict resolution.

Spiritual-Awareness: After our Self-Awareness time, we are going to open our Bibles and dig deep into the promises of God's Word. We are going to study about how God wants to work in our lives and in the lives of those we care about.

Application: After our bible study, we will take some time to work on applying what we have learned. God's Word has a lot to say to us where we are right now, and we are going to learn how to apply that truth to the decisions and actions of our daily lives.

During all of these parts of our meeting, we will have opportunities to minister to each other. God has given each of us the resource of other caring Christians. All through His Word, He reminds us of the valuable ministry we can have to one another, and we are going to see that kind of ministry to each other begin to happen through this group.

What do you think of when you hear the word conflict?

Examples:
- Anger
- Broken relationships
- Wrong for Christians

How would you define conflict?

Conflict is a difference in opinion or purpose that frustrates someone's goals or desires.

Spiritual Awareness Lead–In

When someone opposes or mistreats me, my instinctive reaction is to devote all my energies to defending myself and defeating my opponent. This self-absorbed attitude usually leads to further problems. When I follow my feelings, I am likely to make impulsive decisions that often offend my opponent and make matters worse. Others respond to conflict by trying to escape from it through denial or flight.

What is the best way to counteract our natural tendency?

By focusing on Christ.

"Since, then, you have been raised with Christ, set your hearts on things above, where Christ is seated at the right hand of God. Set your minds on things above, not on earthly things" (Colossians 3:1-2).

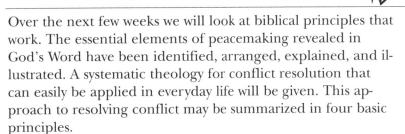

Spiritual-Awareness

Allow 20–25 Minutes

Over the next few weeks we will look at biblical principles that work. The essential elements of peacemaking revealed in God's Word have been identified, arranged, explained, and illustrated. A systematic theology for conflict resolution that can easily be applied in everyday life will be given. This approach to resolving conflict may be summarized in four basic principles.

As you discuss the four principles, ask for volunteers to look up the scripture and read when it is time.

1 Corinthians 10:31
Glorify God — Biblical peacemaking is motivated and directed by a desire to please and honor God. His interests, reputation, and commands should take precedence over all other considerations.

---

from **The Peacemaker's Pledge**

Glorify God — Instead of focusing on our own desires or dwelling on what others may do, we will seek to please and honor God—by depending on His wisdom, power, and love; by faithfully obeying His commands; and by seeking to maintain a loving, merciful, and forgiving attitude.

Describe a situation where you had an opportunity to glorify God in the midst of conflict.

Personal response.

"So whether you eat or drink or whatever you do, do it all for the glory of God" (1 Corinthians 10:31).

Facilitator's Guide: *Peacemaking*, Turning Point, P. O. Box 22127, Chattanooga, TN 37422-2127

Matthew 7:5
Get the log out of your eye — Peacemaking requires facing up to our own attitudes, faults, and responsibilities before pointing out what others have done wrong. Overlooking the minor offenses of others and honestly admitting our own faults often will encourage similar responses from our opponents.

---

from **The Peacemaker's Pledge**

Get the Log out of your own eye — Instead of attacking others or dwelling on their wrongs, we will take responsibility for our own contribution to conflicts—confessing our sins, asking God to help us change any attitudes and habits that lead to conflict, and seeking to repair any harm we have caused.

Are you open to personal examination? Explain.

Personal response.

"First take the plank out of your own eye, and then you will see clearly to remove the speck from your brother's eye" (Matthew 7:5).

Matthew 18:15
Go and show your brother his fault — At times peacemaking also requires constructive confrontation. When others fail to accept responsibility for their actions, we may need to confront them in a gracious yet firm manner.

Give an example of constructive confrontation.

Personal response.

---

from **The Peacemaker's Pledge**

Go and show your brother his fault — Instead of pretending that conflict doesn't exist or talking about others behind their backs, we will choose to overlook minor offenses, or we will talk directly and graciously with those whose offenses seem too serious to overlook. When a conflict with another Christian cannot be resolved in private, we will ask others in the body of Christ to help us settle the matter in a biblical manner.

What benefits do you see in this principle versus "going public" without this process?

Personal response.

"If your brother sins against you, go and show him his fault, just between the two of you. If he listens to you, you have won your brother over (Matthew 18:15).

Matthew 5:24

Go and be reconciled — Finally, peacemaking involves a commitment to restoring damaged relationships and developing agreements that are just and satisfactory to everyone involved. Forgiveness and cooperative negotiation clear away the debris left by conflict and make possible reconciliation and genuine peace.

---

from **The Peacemaker's Pledge**

Go and be reconciled — Instead of accepting premature compromise or allowing relationships to wither, we will actively pursue genuine peace and reconciliation—forgiving others as God, for Christ's sake, has forgiven us, and seeking just and mutually beneficial solutions to our differences.

Reconciliation involves forgiveness. In light of Ephesians 4:32, how are we to forgive others?

We are to forgive as God forgave us.

"First go and be reconciled to your brother; then come and offer your gift" (Matthew 5:24).

Application

Allow 20 Minutes

The more you study and apply God's peacemaking principles, the more you will see how practical and powerful they are. When used properly, these principles can rob conflict of its destructive tendencies and turn it into an opportunity to find lasting solutions to serious problems; to experience significant personal growth; to deepen relationships; and, best of all, to know and enjoy God in a new and vibrant way.

---

from **The Peacemaker's Pledge**

By God's grace, we will apply these principles as a matter of stewardship, realizing that conflict is an assignment, not an accident. We will remember that success, in God's eyes, is not a matter of specific results but of faithful, dependent obedience. And we will pray that our service as peacemakers brings praise to our Lord and leads others to know His infinite love.

Facilitator's Guide: *Peacemaking*, Turning Point, P. O. Box 22127, Chattanooga, TN 37422-2127

Here are some questions we can ask ourselves. Share a brief prayer concerning each of the questions stating your goals and your need for God's help in each area dealing with a present or possible conflict.

Glorify God — How can I please and honor the Lord in this situation?

Get the log out of your eye — How have I contributed to this conflict, and what do I need to do to resolve it?

Go and show your brother his fault — How can I help others to understand how they have contributed to this conflict?

Go and be reconciled — How can I demonstrate forgiveness and encourage a reasonable solution to this conflict?

Closing Prayer

Ask for volunteers to share their prayers as time permits.

Pray that our "love may abound more and more in knowledge and depth of insight, so that [we] may be able to discern what is best and may be pure and blameless until the day of Christ, filled with the fruit of righteousness that comes through Jesus Christ—to the glory and praise of God" (Philippians 1:9-11).

Facilitator's Guide: *Peacemaking*, Turning Point, P. O. Box 22127, Chattanooga, TN 37422-2127

Part I

Glorify God

So whether you eat or drink or whatever you do, do it all for the glory of God.

1 Corinthians 10:31

---

from **The Peacemaker's Pledge**

Glorify God — Instead of focusing on our own desires or dwelling on what others may do, we will seek to please and honor God—by depending on His wisdom, power, and love; by faithfully obeying His commands; and by seeking to maintain a loving, merciful, and forgiving attitude.

Session 1 Conflict Provides Opportunities

"Well done, good and faithful servant!" (Matthew 25:21).

Introduction

Allow 10 Minutes

Opening Prayer

Thank God for faithfully showing us in His Holy Word how to deal with conflict. Pray that each person in the group will be a living testimony to His grace as we follow His example.

Sharing Question

What are some positive and negative ways you can think of to respond to conflict?

Personal response.

Self-Awareness

Allow 20–25 Minutes

This story illustrates how people may have different perspectives regarding a situation or an issue:

Read Chapter 1 and pages 245-251 from *The Peacemaker* for further preparation for this session.

Ask for a volunteer to read the opening story.

In 1986 I was hiking with three friends in the Beartooth Mountains in southern Montana. It was early in the summer, and the streams were still swollen from melting snow. Ten miles into the mountains, we came to a stream where the bridge had been washed away. The water was deep and icy cold. There was one place where we might have been able to cross by leaping from rock to rock, but it would have meant risking a fall into the rapids.

As we stood there trying to decide what to do, three different perspectives surfaced. One person saw the stream as a dangerous obstacle. Afraid that one of us might fall in and be swept away, he wanted to turn back and look for another trail. Another friend saw the stream as a means to show how tough he was. He wanted to wade straight across, even if that meant we would be wet and cold for a few hours. But two of us saw the stream as an interesting challenge. We studied the rocks leading to the other side and determined where we would need additional footing. Finding a fallen tree in the woods, we laid it across the largest gap between the rocks.

At this point, our two friends began to cooperate with us. Working together, we managed to get one person over to the other bank. Then two of us stood on rocks in the middle of the stream and the packs were passed to the other side. One by one, we jumped from rock to rock, receiving support from the person ahead. Before long, we were all on the far bank, and we were perfectly dry and exhilarated by our accomplishment.

People look at conflict in much the same way as the stream was viewed in this story. To some, conflict is a hazard that threatens to sweep them off their feet and leave them bruised and hurting. To others, it is an obstacle that they should conquer quickly and firmly; but a few people have learned that conflict is an opportunity to solve common problems in a way that honors God and offers benefits to those involved. As you will see, the latter view can transform the way you respond to conflict.

The Slippery Slope of Conflict

There are three basic ways people respond to conflict. These responses may be arranged on a curve that resembles a hill. On the left slope of the hill we find the *escape responses* to conflict. On the right side we find the *attack responses.* And in the center we find the *conciliation responses.*

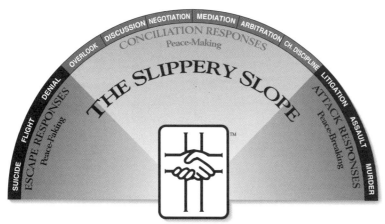

STAYING ON TOP OF CONFLICT

Imagine that this hill is covered with ice. If you go too far to the left or the right, you can lose your footing and slide down the slope. Similarly, when you experience conflict, it is easy to become defensive or antagonistic. Both responses make matters worse and can lead to more extreme reactions.

Fortunately, there are two things you can do to stay on top of this slippery slope: You can learn to resist the natural inclination to escape or attack when faced with conflict, and you can develop the ability to use the conciliation response that is best suited to resolving a particular conflict. Let's look at all the responses in more detail.

Escape Responses

The three responses found on the left side of the slippery slope are called the *escape responses*. People tend to use these responses when they are more interested in avoiding a conflict than in resolving it.

Denial. One way to escape from a conflict is to pretend it does not exist. Another way is to refuse to do what should be done to resolve a conflict properly.

What kind of results have you seen to denial?

These responses bring only temporary relief and usually make matters worse.

Flight. Another way to escape from a conflict is to run away. This may mean ending a friendship, quitting a job, filing for divorce, or changing churches.

What kind of responses have you seen to flight?

Flight may be a legitimate response in extreme circumstances when it is impossible to resolve the conflict in a constructive manner. In most cases, however, running away only postpones a proper solution to a problem.

Suicide. When people lose all hope of resolving a conflict, they may seek to escape the situation (or make a desperate cry for help) by attempting to take their own lives. Suicide is never the right way to deal with conflict. Tragically, however, suicide has become a major cause of death among adolescents in the United States, partly because our children have never learned how to deal with conflict constructively.

Facilitator's Guide: *Peacemaking,* Turning Point, P. O. Box 22127, Chattanooga, TN 37422-2127

Attack Responses

The three responses found on the right side of the slippery slope are called the *attack responses*. These responses are used by people who are more interested in winning a conflict than in preserving a relationship. This attitude is seen in people who view conflict as a contest or an opportunity to assert their rights, to control others, and to take advantage of their situation.

Litigation. Some conflicts may legitimately be taken before a civil judge for a decision; however, only after all other courses of action with church assistance have been exhausted.

What kind of results have you seen from litigation?

Lawsuits usually damage relationships. They often fail to achieve complete justice.

Assault. Some people try to overcome an opponent by using various forms of force or intimidation.

What kinds of force or intimidation have you seen?

Examples:
- Verbal attacks (including gossip and slander)
- Physical violence
- Efforts to damage a person financially or professionally.

Murder. In extreme cases, people may be so desperate to win a dispute that they will try to kill those who oppose them.

Do you think believers view murder differently than non-believers? Describe.

Personal response.

While most Christians would not kill someone, we should never forget that we stand guilty of murder in God's eyes when we harbor contempt in our hearts toward others. See Matthew 5:21-22.

Conciliation Responses

The six responses found on the top portion of the slippery slope are called the *conciliation responses*. These responses are specifically commended by God and directed toward finding just and mutually agreeable solutions to conflict.

Overlook an offense. Many disputes are so insignificant that they should be resolved by quietly and deliberately overlooking an offense and forgiving the person who has wronged you.

Discussion. If a personal offense is too serious to overlook, it should be resolved through confession or loving confrontation.

Negotiation. Substantive issues related to money, property, or other rights should be resolved through a bargaining process during which the parties seek to reach a settlement that satisfies the legitimate needs of each side.

Mediation. If two Christians cannot reach an agreement in private, they should ask one or more others to meet with them to help them communicate more effectively and explore possible solutions.

Arbitration. When you and an opponent cannot come to a voluntary agreement on a substantive issue, you should appoint one or more arbitrators to listen to your arguments and render a binding decision to settle the matter.

Church discipline. If a person who professes to be a Christian refuses to be reconciled and do what is right, his or her church leaders should be asked to formally intervene to promote repentance, justice, and forgiveness.

What is the difference between denial and overlooking an offense?

Denial is pretending a conflict does not exist. Overlooking acknowledges a difference exists and involves making a choice to forgive the offense—just between you and God.

Interesting Trends on the Slope

The slippery slope reveals several interesting trends regarding the various responses to conflict. As we move from the left side of the slope to the right (clockwise), our responses tend to go from being private to being public. When we fail to resolve a matter through a private response, more people must get involved as we look to mediation, arbitration, church discipline, or potential litigation to settle a dispute.

Moving from left to right on the curve also involves a move from consensual to coercive solutions. In all the responses on the left side of the curve, the parties decide on their own solution. In arbitration, church discipline, and the attack responses, a result is imposed by others. This is usually less palatable to everyone involved.

Facilitator's Guide: *Peacemaking*, Turning Point, P. O. Box 22127, Chattanooga, TN 37422-2127

Spiritual Awareness Lead–In

The Bible does not teach that all conflict is bad; instead, it teaches that some differences are natural and beneficial. Many of our differences are not inherently right or wrong; they are simply the result of God-given diversity and personal preferences. When handled properly, disagreements in these areas can stimulate productive dialogue, encourage creativity, promote helpful change, and generally make life more interesting.

Not all conflict is neutral or beneficial, however. The Bible teaches that many disagreements are the direct result of sinful motives and behavior.

James asks the question (James 4:1-2), "What causes fights and quarrels among you?" What is his response?

"Don't they [fights and quarrels] come from your desires that battle within you? You want something but don't get it. You kill and covet, but you cannot have what you want. You quarrel and fight."

Spiritual-Awareness

Allow 20–25 Minutes

Let us look at scriptures that speak to conciliation. The first three conciliation responses discussed in Self-Awareness may be referred to as *personal peacemaking* because they may be carried out personally and privately, just between you and the other party.

Ask for volunteers to look up scripture and read when it is time.

Proverbs 19:11; Proverbs 17:14
Many insignificant disputes should be overlooked. How is this beneficial and preventative to further harm?

"It is to his glory to overlook an offense"

"Starting a quarrel is like breaching a dam; so drop the matter before a dispute breaks out."

Matthew 5:23-24, 18:15
Discussion is often necessary when a personal issue cannot be overlooked. Who should be involved in this discussion?

You and your brother or sister. The offended and the offender.

Philippians 2:4
Substantive issues may call for negotiations. How should each party approach the legitimate needs of each other?

"Each of you should look not only to your own interests, but also to the interests of others."

When a dispute cannot be resolved through one of the personal peacemaking responses, you should use one of the three assisted responses. These require the involvement of other people from your church or community.

Matthew 18:16 Sometimes Christians cannot reach an agreement in private. If this is the case, what should they do?	Use mediators. "But if he will not listen, take one or two others along, so that 'every matter may be established by the testimony of two or three witnesses.' "
1 Corinthians 6:1-8 When parties cannot come to a voluntary agreement, one or more arbitrators should be appointed to render a binding decision. How should Christians resolve legal conflicts with one another?	"If you have disputes about such matters, appoint as judges even men of little account in the church!" (v 4).
Matthew 18:17 Sometimes church discipline is necessary. What is the prerequisite for this?	The steps set forth in Matthew 18:15-16.

The Bible teaches that we should see conflict neither as an inconvenience nor as an occasion for selfish gain but rather as an opportunity to demonstrate the presence and power of God.

Application

Allow 20 Minutes

When a person earnestly pursues the conciliation responses to conflict, there is a greater likelihood that he or she will eventually experience or achieve reconciliation. In contrast, both the escape and attack responses to conflict almost inevitably result in KYRG: **K**iss **Y**our **R**elationship **G**ood-bye.

Where are you or have you been on the Slippery Slope? Circle and describe.

STAYING ON TOP OF CONFLICT

Facilitator's Guide: *Peacemaking*, Turning Point, P. O. Box 22127, Chattanooga, TN 37422-2127

Where do you want to be? Describe.

Additional Scripture References		
Genesis 16:6-8	*Matthew 5:21-22*	*Romans 13:1-5*
1 Samuel 2:22-25	*Matthew 5:25-26*	*Galatians 6:1-3*
1 Samuel 19:9-10	*Acts 6:8-15*	*Colossians 3:13*
1 Samuel 31:4	*Acts 7:54-58*	*1 Peter 4:8*
Proverbs 28:13	*Acts 24:1-26*	

Closing Prayer

Remember any specific needs that have been shared. Pray for courage for each individual as we face the challenges of life. Pray that we may grow in our ability to see things from an eternal perspective.

"If it is possible, as far as it depends on you, live at peace with everyone" (Romans 12:18).

Introduction

Allow 10 Minutes

Opening Prayer

Thank God for the faithfulness of each group member. Pray that the Lord will provide a greater insight into what it means to "live at peace with everyone."

Sharing Question

How do you view peacemaking as a matter of stewardship?

Whenever we are involved in a conflict, God has given us an opportunity to manage ourselves in a way that will glorify Him, benefit others, and allow us to grow in character.

Self-Awareness

Allow 20–25 Minutes

The following is a story that shows the importance of living at peace:

Read Chapter 2 from *The Peacemaker* for further preparation for this session.

Ask for a volunteer to read the opening story.

The pastor of a church I attended during college clearly understood the importance of seeking peace with an estranged brother. He demonstrated this the Sunday I brought a friend named Cindy to church for the first time. Thinking that she might find meaningful instruction and encouragement from my church, I had invited her to worship with me one Sunday.

I was unprepared for what took place shortly after Cindy and I took our seats because I had forgotten that during the previous week's Sunday school period, my pastor and an elder had gotten into a public argument. Pastor Woods called for the attention of the congregation and asked the elder with whom he had quarreled to join him at the pulpit. "As most of you know," Pastor Woods said, "Kent and I had an argument during Sunday school last week. Our emotions got out of hand, and we said some things that should have been discussed in private."

As I thought of the first impression Cindy must be getting, my stomach sank. "Of all of the days to bring someone to church," I thought, "why did I pick this one?" I was sure this incident would discourage Cindy from coming to my church again.

Pastor Woods put his arm around Kent's shoulders and went on. "We want you to know that we met that same afternoon to resolve our differences. By God's grace, we came to understand each other better, and we were fully reconciled. We need to tell you how sorry we are for disrupting the unity of this fellowship, and we ask for your forgiveness for the poor testimony we gave last week."

Many eyes were filled with tears as Pastor Woods and Kent prayed together. Unfortunately, I was so worried about what Cindy might be thinking that I completely missed the significance of what had happened. Making a nervous comment to Cindy, I opened the hymnal to our first song and hoped she would forget about the whole incident. The rest of the service was a blur, and before long, I was driving her home. I made light conversation for a few minutes, but eventually Cindy referred to what had happened: "I still can't believe what your pastor did this morning. I've never met a minister in my church who had the courage and humility to do what he did. I'd like to come to your church again."

During subsequent visits, Cindy's respect for my pastor and for Kent continued to grow; and before long, she made our church her spiritual home. She saw real evidence of God's presence and power in those two men. Their humility highlighted God's strength and helped Cindy to take Christ more seriously. As a result, she committed herself to Christ and began to grow in her faith.

What impresses you the most about this story?

> When we accept the responsibility of handling conflict as a matter of stewardship, we will manage ourselves in a way that will glorify God, minister to others, and grow us in character.

Jesus' Reputation Depends on Unity

When peace and unity characterize your relationships with other people, you know God is present in your life. The converse is also true. When your life is filled with unresolved conflict, you will have little success in sharing the Good News about Jesus Christ. This principle is taught repeatedly throughout the New Testament.

One of the most emphatic statements on peace and unity in the Bible is found in Jesus' prayer shortly before he was arrested and taken away to be crucified. After praying for himself and for unity among his disciples (John 17:1-9), Jesus prayed for all who would someday believe in him. These words apply directly to every Christian today.

Describe the responsibility you feel for unity.

The way I deal with conflict will affect issues of unity and subsequently Jesus' reputation.

Lawsuits among Believers

When Paul learned that Christians in Corinth were suing one another in secular courts, he was dismayed. Because he knew that lawsuits between Christians were inconsistent with Jesus' teachings and would do serious damage to the witness of the church, he sharply rebuked the Corinthians. (See 1 Corinthians 6:1-8.)

When Christians cannot resolve their differences privately, God commands that we turn to the church rather than to the civil courts. Many churches ignore this passage and do nothing to help Christians settle their disputes in a biblical manner. This failure was specifically noted by Chief Justice Warren Burger in 1982.

> One reason our courts have become overburdened is that Americans are increasingly turning to the courts for relief from a range of personal distresses and anxieties. Remedies for personal wrongs that once were considered the responsibility of institutions other than the courts are now boldly asserted as legal "entitlements." The courts have been expected to fill the void created by the decline of church, family, and neighborhood unity (p. 68).

What is your impression of Chief Justice Burger's statement?

Personal response.

The church's neglect in fulfilling its traditional peacemaking responsibilities has deprived Christians of valuable assistance; contributed to the congestion of our court system; and, worst of all, damaged the witness of Christ. Fortunately, there are still some Christians who take Paul's rebuke seriously. For example, Associate Supreme Court Justice Antonin Scalia made this observation:

Facilitator's Guide: *Peacemaking*, Turning Point, P. O. Box 22127, Chattanooga, TN 37422-2127

I think this passage (1 Corinthians 6:1-8) has something to say about the proper Christian attitude toward civil litigation. Paul is making two points: First, he says that the mediation of a mutual friend, such as the parish priest, should be sought before parties run off to the law courts. . . . I think we are too ready today to seek vindication or vengeance through adversary proceedings rather than peace through mediation. . . . Good Christians, just as they are slow to anger, should be slow to sue (pp. 8-9).

What do you think about Associate Supreme Court Justice Antonin Scalia's statement, "Good Christians, just as they are slow to anger, should be slow to sue"?

Personal response.

Spiritual Awareness Lead–In

Nothing reveals God's concern for peace more vividly than His decision to send His beloved Son to "guide our feet into the path of peace" (Luke 1:79; cf. Isaiah 2:4). From beginning to end, Jesus' mission was one of peacemaking. Long before He was born, He was given a title.

What was the title (Isaiah 9:6)?

"Prince of Peace"

Spiritual-Awareness

Allow 20–25 Minutes

The Bible teaches that God is deeply interested in peace.

There are three dimensions to the peace God offers to us through Christ: peace with God, peace with one another, and peace within ourselves. Many people care little about their relationships with God and other people; all they want is peace within themselves. As you will see, it is impossible to know genuine internal peace unless you also pursue peace with God and others.

The Three Dimensions of Peace

Peace with God

Isaiah 59:1-2
Peace with God does not come automatically since all of us have sinned and alienated ourselves from Him.

What hope does verse 1 provide?

"Surely the arm of the LORD is not too short to save."

Romans 3:23-24
Each of us has a record stained with sin. Describe the universal aspect of this verse.

"For all have sinned and fall short of the glory of God." This includes all people.

What hope does verse 24 provide?

We can be "justified freely by his grace through the redemption that came by Christ Jesus."

John 3:16
This verse provides good news. Describe the universal aspect of this verse.

"Whoever believes in him shall not perish but have eternal life."

This good news is for everyone (whoever).

Romans 5:1-2
By sacrificing himself on the cross, Jesus has made it possible for us to have peace with God.

How do we gain access into His grace?

By faith.

Believing in Jesus means trusting that He exchanged records with you at Calvary—that is, He took your sinful record on himself and paid for it in full, giving you his perfect record which opens the way for peace with God.

Peace with Others

Ephesians 2:11-18
In addition to giving us peace with God, Jesus' sacrifice on the cross opened the way for us to enjoy peace with other people.

Verse 14 describes the origin of our peace with others. Who is it?

"For he himself [Christ] is our peace."

How does this reconciliation with God and others come? (See verses 15 and 16.)

We are reconciled to God and with others through the cross.

Psalm 133:1
This peace, which is often referred to as *unity*, is not simply the absence of conflict and strife.

Describe the good news of this verse.

It is "good and pleasant . . . when brothers live together in unity!"

God commands us to do all we can to "live at peace with everyone" whether or not they are Christians (Romans 12:18).

Peace within Ourselves

Isaiah 32:17
Internal peace is a by-product of righteousness.
What is the fruit of righteousness?

Peace.

What is the effect of righteousness?

"Quietness and confidence forever."

Isaiah 48:18
We should give attention to God's commands.
In view of this verse, why is this important?

"Your peace [will be] like a river, your righteousness like the waves of the sea."

If you want to experience internal peace, you must seek harmonious relationships with God and others.

Facilitator's Guide: *Peacemaking*, Turning Point, P. O. Box 22127, Chattanooga, TN 37422-2127   **Session 2**   **25**

The Enemy of Peace

Since peace and unity are essential to an effective Christian witness, you can be sure there is one who will do all he can to promote conflict and division within the fellowship of believers. Satan, whose name means "adversary," likes nothing better than to see us at odds with one another. "Your enemy the devil prowls around like a roaring lion looking for someone to devour" (1 Peter 5:8b).

Satan promotes conflict in many ways. Among other things, he fills our hearts with greed and dishonesty (Acts 5:3), deceives us as to what will make us happy (2 Timothy 2:25-26), and takes advantage of unresolved anger (Ephesians 4:26-27). Worst of all, he uses false teachers to propagate values and philosophies that encourage selfishness and stimulate controversy (1 Timothy 4:1-3).

Application

Allow 20 Minutes

The message given by Jesus and the apostles is resoundingly clear: Whether our conflicts involve minor irritations or major legal issues, peace and unity are of paramount importance to God. Therefore, peacemaking is not an optional activity for a believer. If you have committed your life to Christ, He commands you to make peace and unity a high priority in your life. Token efforts will not satisfy this command. God wants you to strive earnestly, diligently, and continually to maintain harmonious relationships with those around you. Your obedience to this call will advance the gospel and allow you to enjoy the personal peace God gives to those who faithfully serve Him.

If you are presently involved in a conflict, these questions will help you to apply the principles presented in this session.

Have you made peace with God by accepting Jesus Christ as your Savior, Lord, and King? If not, you can do so right now by sincerely praying this prayer:

> Lord Jesus,
>   I know I am a sinner, and I realize my good deeds could never make up for my wrongs. I need your forgiveness. I believe you died for my sins, and I want to turn away from them. I trust you now to be my Savior, and I will follow you as my Lord and King in the fellowship of your church.

   Facilitator's Guide: *Peacemaking,* Turning Point, P. O. Box 22127, Chattanooga, TN 37422-2127

If you have prayed this prayer, it is essential that you find fellowship with other Christians in a church where the Bible is faithfully taught and applied. This fellowship will help you to learn more about God and to be strengthened in your faith.

As time permits, ask for volunteers to share one or more of the questions. Also, include the prayer.

❶   Are you at peace with other people? If not, from whom are you estranged? Why?

❷   Are you experiencing the kind of internal peace you desire? If not, why?

❸   Have the peace and unity of the Christian community been disrupted by your dispute? How?

❹   What effect might this conflict be having on the reputation of Christ?

❺   Is there someone who might have something against you? What have you done to be reconciled? Do you believe you are free to worship God, or do you need to make another effort to restore unity with that person?

❻   Go on record with the Lord by writing a prayer based on the principles taught in this session.

Additional Scripture References

Psalm 85:10	*John 17:1-19*	*1 Thessalonians 5:13-15*
Psalm 119:165	*1Corinthians 1:10*	*James 4:7*
Isaiah 26:3	*Ephesians 2:17*	*1 Peter 5:8*
Matthew 5:9	*Ephesians 6:12*	*1 John 3:23*
Matthew 22:39	*Colossians 1:19-20*	
John 14:27	*Colossians 3:13,15*	

Closing Prayer

Pray for the needs you heard expressed during the meeting. Be sure to invite others to pray as well.

Session 3 Trust in the Lord and Do Good

"The LORD's unfailing love surrounds the man who trusts in him" (Psalm 32:10).

Introduction

Allow 10 Minutes

Opening Prayer

> Thank God for each member present. Ask for His wisdom and insight as we study peacemaking.

Sharing Questions

What do you fear most about conflict?

> Personal response.

Self-Awareness

Allow 20-25 Minutes

The more you trust God, the easier it is to do His will. This is especially true when you are involved in conflict. If you believe God is watching over you with perfect love and unlimited power, you will be able to serve Him faithfully as a peacemaker, even in the most difficult circumstances.

> Read Chapter 3 from *The Peacemaker* for further preparation for this session.

God has continued to provide us with examples of the kind of trust that honors him. One of the most profound examples in recent years was given by Jim and Elisabeth Elliot. In 1956, Jim and four other missionaries were murdered when they tried to carry the gospel to the Aucas, an isolated tribe in South America. Elisabeth was deeply grieved by the loss of her husband, and she had to wrestle through many unanswered questions. As this excerpt from her subsequent book reveals, she continued to trust in the sovereignty of God:

> To the world at large this was a sad waste of five young lives. But God has his plan and purpose in all things. . . . The prayers of the widows themselves are for the Aucas. We look forward to the day when these savages will join us in Christian praise. Plans were promptly formulated for continuing the work of the martyrs (Elliott, pp. 252-254).

The widows carried on the work their husbands had begun. Three years after the killings, God answered their prayers and began to open Auca hearts to the gospel. Even some of the men who had killed the five missionaries eventually came

Facilitator's Guide: *Peacemaking,* Turning Point, P. O. Box 22127, Chattanooga, TN 37422-2127

to Christ. Although Elisabeth praised God for the conversions He brought about, she acknowledged they were not the sole measure of God's purpose in her husband's death. In 1981, she added an epilogue to her book which included these words:

> The Auca story . . . has pointed to one thing: God is God. If He is God, he is worthy of my worship, and my service. I will find rest nowhere but in his will, and that will is infinitely, immeasurably, unspeakably beyond my largest notions of what he is up to. God is the God of human history, and he is at work continuously, mysteriously, accomplishing his eternal purposes in us, through us, for us, and in spite of us. . . . Cause and effect are in God's hands. Is it not the part of faith simply to let them rest there? God *is* God. I dethrone him in my heart if I demand that he act in ways that satisfy my idea of justice. . . . The one who laid the earth's foundations and settled its dimensions knows where the lines are drawn. He gives all the light we need for trust and obedience (Elliott, pp. 268-269, 273).

What was it that allowed these missionaries to keep going in spite of these challenges?

Among other things, they had the humility to recognize the limits of their own understanding and the wisdom to bow before God's eternal purposes. Through prayer, study, and experience, they learned to trust completely in the sovereignty of God.

Although we can be sure God is always working for our good and the good of others, even through trials and suffering, we will not always know exactly what that good is. In many cases His ultimate purposes will not be evident for a long time. In other situations His ways and objectives are simply too profound for us to comprehend, at least until we see God face-to-face. Trusting God means that *in spite of our questions, doubts, and fears,* we draw on His grace and continue to believe that God is loving, that He is in control, and that He is always working for good. Such trust helps us to continue doing what is good and right, even in difficult circumstances.

The Bible is filled with examples of people who experienced all kinds of misgivings and yet continued to trust in God. For example, when Job suffered incredible hardship, he voiced many doubts and apprehensions. Even so, he eventually understood that God's plan could not be thwarted. (See Job 42:2-3.)

Describe a trust issue in your life that has reminded you of Job.

Personal response.

Spiritual Awareness Lead–In

The Apostle Paul had the same habit of trusting God regardless of his circumstances. In Philippi, he and Silas were falsely accused, severely flogged, and thrown into prison. Incredibly, instead of wallowing in doubt or despair, they spent the night "praying and singing hymns to God" (Acts 16:25).

How did God respond in this conflict?

By bringing about an earthquake, the conversion of the jailer and his family, and an apology from the city officials. See Acts 16:16-40.

Spiritual-Awareness

Allow 20-25 Minutes

One reason Jesus and Paul trusted God so completely was that they knew He was in complete control of everything that happened in their lives. This perfect control is often referred to as "the sovereignty of God." The Bible provides many examples of people who trusted God even in the midst of terrible hardship and suffering.

Matthew 26:42; Luke 23:46; 1 Peter 2:23
Jesus was faced with the horror of the cross.

What was Jesus' primary focus in these verses?

Trust in God
"May your will be done" (Matthew 26:42).

"Father, into your hands I commit my spirit" (Luke 23:46).

"He entrusted himself to him who judges justly" (1 Peter 2:23).

2 Timothy 1:12
The Apostle Paul responded to his imprisonment, suffering, and impending execution in a manner that showed trust in God.

Describe this trust in your own words.

He knew why he was suffering (for the cause of Christ). He was not ashamed of his difficulties. He was convinced that God was able to guard what he had "entrusted to him for that day."

Isaiah 46:9-10
God is sovereign. To be sovereign means to be supreme, unlimited, and totally independent of any other influence.

Facilitator's Guide: *Peacemaking*, Turning Point, P. O. Box 22127, Chattanooga, TN 37422-2127

How do these verses describe God's sovereignty?	We are reminded that God was there in the past and He is without compare. He spans the total time frame—"I make known the end from the beginning, from ancient times, what is still to come. . . . My purpose will stand" (v 10).
Psalm 135:6-7; Colossians 1:16-17 God's sovereignty extends over both creation and preservation. In light of Colossians 1:17, how does God prevent creation from becoming chaotic?	"In him all things hold together."
Proverbs 21:1; Daniel 2:20, 4:35 God rules over all governments. What in Daniel 4:35 shows His unlimited powers in heaven and on earth?	"No one can hold back his hand or say to him: 'What have you done?' "
Jeremiah 18:6; Ephesians 1:11-12; James 4:13-15 He alone controls individual lives and destinies. James 4:13-15 describes different aspects of one's life—determination, time, business, and economy. What important statement should always be a part of life decisions and choices?	"If it is the Lord's will, we will live and do this or that" (James 4:15).
Ezekiel 33:11; James 1:13-14 God takes no pleasure in what is hurtful, and He is never the author of sin. Yet for His eternal purposes, He sometimes allows suffering and permits unjust acts by men and women—He decides not to restrain even though He has the power to do so. Jesus' death on the cross is an example of His restraint in order to accomplish His plan of redemption. What in James 1:13 shows us that Jesus is not the author of sin? God exercises ultimate control and works things out for His good purposes. At the right time, God will administer justice and right all wrongs. See Proverbs 16:4-5.	"For God cannot be tempted by evil, nor does he tempt anyone."

Matthew 12:36
The fact that God has ultimate control does not release us from responsibility for our actions.

Describe the accountability in this verse.

"[We] will have to give an account on the day of judgment for every careless word [we] have spoken."

Psalm 62:11-12
The foundation for our trust in God is found in these verses.

What are they?

His strength and love.

If all we knew was that God is in control, we could have reason to fear. Indeed, if He used His power arbitrarily, sometimes for good and sometimes for evil, we would be in great danger; but this is not the case. God is good—His power is always wielded with perfect love.

Trust Is a Decision

Your view of God will have a profound effect on how much you trust Him. If you do not believe He is both sovereign and good, trust will be an elusive thing for a god who is loving but not in control is simply "a heavenly Santa Claus . . . who means well, but cannot always insulate his children from trouble and grief" (Packer, p. 145). Such a god offers little security or hope in the face of affliction and fails to inspire either trust or obedience.

On the other hand, if you believe God is sovereign and good, you will be able to trust and obey Him even in the midst of difficult circumstances. See Proverbs 3:5-6.

Application

Allow 20 Minutes

When you are involved in a conflict, you must decide whether or not you will trust God. Trusting God does not mean believing that He will do all that you want, but rather that He will do everything He knows is good. If you do not trust God, you will inevitably place your trust in yourself or someone else which ultimately leads to grief. On the other hand, if you believe God is sovereign and that He will never let anything into your life unless it can be used for good, you will see conflicts not as accidents but as assignments. This kind of trust glorifies God and inspires the faithfulness needed for effective peacemaking.

 Facilitator's Guide: *Peacemaking,* Turning Point, P. O. Box 22127, Chattanooga, TN 37422-2127

If you are presently involved in a conflict, these questions will help you to apply the principles presented in this session.

As time permits, ask for volunteers to share one or more of the questions. Also include the prayer.

❶   Have you been looking at this conflict as something that happened by chance, as something done to you by someone else, or as something God allowed in your life for a specific purpose? Describe.

❷   What questions, doubts, or fears do you have because of this conflict? Describe.

❸   How would your feelings, attitude, and behavior change if you started seeing this conflict as an assignment from a perfectly loving and all-powerful God? Describe.

❹   What good might God bring about if you respond to this conflict in a biblical manner? Describe.

❺   Go on record with the Lord by writing a prayer based on the principles taught in this session.

Additional Scripture References

Exodus 4:10-12	*Isaiah 43:2-3*	*Romans 8:28-29*
Job 1:6-12	*Matthew 10:29-31*	*Romans 9:15-16*
Job 42:11	*John 1:3*	*Romans 15:32*
Psalm 71:20-21	*John 6:39*	*2 Corinthians 1:9*
Proverbs 16:9	*John 9:1-5*	*James 1:2-4*
Proverbs 16:33	*John 11:1-4*	*Revelation 4:11*
Proverbs 19:21	*Acts 2:23*	

Closing Prayer

Pray for any specific needs group members may express concerning conflict issues. Pray for encouragement and wisdom for the group.

Part II

Get the Log Out
of Your Eye

**You hypocrite, first take the plank out of
your own eye, and then you will see
clearly to remove the speck from
your brother's eye.**
Matthew 7:5

---

from **The Peacemaker's Pledge**

Get the Log out of your own eye — Instead of attacking others or
dwelling on their wrongs, we will take responsibility for our own
contribution to conflicts—confessing our sins, asking God to
help us change any attitudes and habits that lead to conflict,
and seeking to repair any harm we have caused.

Session 4 · *Is This Really Worth Fighting Over?*

"A man's wisdom gives him patience; it is to his glory to overlook an offense" (Proverbs 19:11).

Introduction

Allow 10 Minutes

Opening Prayer

> Thank God for the group members who have been faithful in coming and allowing God to work in their lives. Ask for His guidance and wisdom as we approach the subject—Is This Really Worth Fighting Over?

Sharing Questions

What spiritual discipline do you find the easiest or the most difficult?

> Examples:
> - Prayer
> - Bible study
> - Worship
> - Practicing self-sacrificing love

Self-Awareness

Allow 20-25 Minutes

The following story illustrates "Is This Really Worth Fighting Over?"

> Read Chapter 4 from *The Peacemaker* for further preparation for this session.
>
> Ask for a volunteer to read the opening story.

I was once asked to help four partners divide the assets of a business. One of the men wanted much more than the other three were willing to give him. It was soon evident that the one partner was not going to participate in a negotiation process. If he could not have the share he demanded and believed was rightfully his, he was going to file a lawsuit. For several weeks the other partners had firmly refused to concede to his demands. When I met with those three and asked them why they would not settle, they said, "It isn't just the money; it's the principle of the matter."

In response, I asked, "How much is this principle costing you? How much time has this dispute already taken away from your business, and how much time will a lawsuit consume? More importantly, what effect has this conflict had on you personally and on your families?" There was a long pause, and then one of the

Facilitator's Guide: *Peacemaking*, Turning Point, P. O. Box 22127, Chattanooga, TN 37422-2127

partners pulled out his calculator. After a few key strokes, he said, "I'd say we have already lost over two thousand dollars in billable time. A lawsuit could easily cost us ten times that amount." Then one of the other partners admitted he had not been sleeping well because of the tensions created by the conflict. He also conceded that his critical attitude had created problems with his wife and children. The third partner made a similar comment.

When these three men added up the real cost of their dispute and compared it to the cost of settling the matter, they saw that the wisest thing to do would be to settle the matter as quickly as possible. Although it was difficult for them to do at the time, one of them later told me that within two weeks of the settlement, he was completely free of the matter. "When I look back," he said, "I have a hard time understanding why we didn't settle it much earlier. It sure wasn't worth all that fighting."

Have you ever used the statement in the story—"It isn't just the money [or whatever]; it's the principle of the matter"?

Describe.

Personal response.

As long as a disagreement is unresolved, there is the potential for further damage to a relationship. This is one of the reasons for Jesus' command to settle disputes, even lawsuits, as quickly as possible: "Settle matters quickly with your adversary who is taking you to court" (Matthew 5:25).

Unresolved conflict can lead to several types of "prisons" and exact a variety of prices. In some cases you may lose money or property if you do not settle a dispute voluntarily. At other times you may lose your good reputation in your community as a result of continuous negative gossip or publicity. Worst of all, you may get caught in a prison of bitterness.

Some people resist overlooking offenses and forgiving others by arguing, "I have my rights—and it wouldn't be *just* to let him off so easily."

Much of what is legal today is not "right" when viewed from a biblical perspective. As Supreme Court Justice Antonin Scalia has noted:

> What is lawful is not always right. Confusing the two concepts is particularly easy for the English-speaking because we use the word "right" to refer both to legality and to moral appropriateness. . . . We say, "I have a *right* to plead the Fifth Amendment and refuse to answer questions

about possible criminal activity"—even when the consequences of exercising that "right" may cause an innocent person to be convicted. Exercising such a "right" is certainly wrong (p. 9).

Many conflicts arise or grow because people use legal rights wrongly. Give an example.

Examples:
- Some people avoid moral obligations or liabilities by pleading the statute of frauds or the statute of limitations.
- Others reap windfalls from less powerful people by rigidly enforcing certain business advantages.

When exercising a "right" allows you to avoid a moral responsibility or to take unfair advantage of others, you have not acted justly, regardless of what a court might say. Therefore, you should always strive to exercise only those rights that will pass both a legal and a heavenly review. The basic principle to follow at all times is to "do to others what you would have them do to you" (Matthew 7:12).

On the other hand, the Bible teaches that it is sometimes appropriate to exercise our rights, to confront others, and to hold them fully accountable for their responsibilities and their wrongs. For example, Paul quickly asserted his rights as a Roman citizen to avoid a flogging and also to secure an appeal of his case (Acts 22:25-29, 25:11).

Here again the concept of stewardship serves as a guiding principle. Rights are simply privileges given to you by God, and He wants you to use them for His glory. A secondary concern should be how exercising your rights can be of benefit to others, especially by helping them to know Christ.

Facilitator's Guide: *Peacemaking*, Turning Point, P. O. Box 22127, Chattanooga, TN 37422-2127

Spiritual Awareness Lead–In

Jesus had much to say about resolving conflict. One of His most famous commands is recorded in Matthew 7:3-5:

> Why do you look at the speck of sawdust in your brother's eye and pay no attention to the plank in your own eye? How can you say to your brother, "Let me take the speck out of your eye," when all the time there is a plank in your own eye? You hypocrite, first take the plank out of your own eye, and then you will see clearly to remove the speck from your brother's eye.

This passage is sometimes interpreted as forbidding us to confront others about their faults.

Do you think that is a correct interpretation of this passage? Describe.

This passage does not forbid confrontation. Rather, it forbids premature and improper confrontation. Before you talk to others about their faults, you need to face up to yours. Once you have dealt with your contribution to a conflict, you may approach others about theirs.

Spiritual-Awareness

Allow 20-25 Minutes

One of the first things to do when you are involved in a conflict is to define the personal and material issues and discern how they relate to one another. Material issues involve substantive matters. Personal issues are those things going on inside of you or between persons. It is usually wise to begin this process by asking yourself, "Is this really worth fighting over?" When significant personal or material issues are involved, the answer to this question will be yes, and you will need to follow the steps described in subsequent sessions. In many cases, however, if you look at the situation from a biblical perspective, the answer will be no which means you should settle the matter as quickly and quietly as possible. Below are some of the principles that will help you answer this question properly.

Overlook Minor Offenses

In many situations, the best way to resolve a conflict is simply to overlook the offenses of another.

Proverbs 19:11; Proverbs 12:16
Patience is an important quality in overlooking minor offenses.

What qualities should a person pursue in order to overlook such offenses?	Wisdom and prudence.
Proverbs 17:14 Starting a dispute is like breaking through a dam. How is this to be avoided?	"Drop the matter before a dispute breaks out."
1 Peter 4:8 We are encouraged to "love each other deeply." Why is this important in overlooking minor offenses?	"Because love covers over a multitude of sins."

When we overlook the wrongs that others commit against us, we are imitating God's extraordinary forgiveness toward us: "The LORD is compassionate and gracious, slow to anger, abounding in love. He will not always accuse, nor will he harbor his anger forever; he does not treat us as our sins deserve or repay us according to our iniquities" (Psalm 103:8-10).

When considering whether to overlook an offense or not, there are three questions you can ask that may be helpful. Is the offense:
- Dishonoring to God?
- Permanently damaging to your relationship?
- Harmful to others or the offender?

More on this in Session 7.

Check Your Attitude—And Change It

When someone has wronged you and you are still feeling frustrated or hurt, it is difficult to overlook the offense. It is even more difficult if you are overly sensitive to the wrongs of others and tend to dwell excessively on what they have done. One way to guard against this problem is to check your attitude in the light of God's Word.

Paul's letter to the Philippians contains an excellent formula for examining one's attitudes during a conflict. Apparently Paul had heard that two friends in Philippi were having an argument. It must have been a significant one because word of it had crossed the sea and reached Paul in prison. Therefore, as part of his open letter to the church at Philippi, Paul took the time to urge these two women to seek peace:

> I plead with Euodia and I plead with Syntyche to agree with each other in the Lord. Yes, and I ask you, loyal yoke-fellow, help these women who have contended at my side

Facilitator's Guide: *Peacemaking*, Turning Point, P. O. Box 22127, Chattanooga, TN 37422-2127

in the cause of the gospel, along with Clement and the rest of my fellow workers, whose names are in the book of life.

Rejoice in the Lord always. I will say it again: Rejoice! Let your gentleness be evident to all. The Lord is near. Do not be anxious about anything, but in everything, by prayer and petition, with thanksgiving, present your requests to God. And the peace of God, which transcends all understanding, will guard your hearts and your minds in Christ Jesus.

Finally, brothers, whatever is true, whatever is noble, whatever is right, whatever is pure, whatever is lovely, whatever is admirable—if anything is excellent or praise worthy—think about such things. Whatever you have learned or received or heard from me, or seen in me—put it into practice. And the God of peace will be with you (Philippians 4:2-9).

Paul has broken his instructions into five basic principles which you also can use whenever you are involved in a conflict.

❶ Rejoice in the Lord always (v 4).

Paul urges us to be God-centered in our approach to conflict. Moreover, he wants us to be joyfully God-centered.

How does he emphasize this point?

> By repeating it. "Rejoice in the Lord always. I will say it again: Rejoice!"

What is there to rejoice about when you are involved in a dispute?

> - You can rejoice that your trust is in Christ.
> - You can rejoice that you have received forgiveness through Christ.
> - You can rejoice that God is in control.

❷ Let your gentleness be evident to all (v 5).

What does this passage say to you?

> Example:
> - It is describing a quality which is the opposite of irritability, rudeness, and abrasiveness.
> - It is describing a quality that would make a person nice instead of nasty.

❸   Replace anxiety with prayer (v 6).

How does replacing anxiety with prayer bring relief in difficult situations?

When you place your focus on God through prayer, you can begin to experience something that does not seem logical: The hostility, anxiety, and inner conflict with which you have been dealing will begin to give way to a peace that Paul says "transcends all understanding" (v 7).

❹   See things as they really are (v 8).

How do you see verse 8 being an outgrowth of verse 7?

As you replace anxiety with prayer, you will be ready to follow Paul's fourth instruction which is to develop a more accurate view of your opponent and the situation.

The best way to overcome your prejudicial tendency is to think deliberately about aspects of your opponent that are true, noble, right, pure, lovely, admirable—in short, "excellent, or praiseworthy." Paul is not saying we should think only about the good things in others for he clearly understands the necessity of confronting sin and encouraging repentance (Galatians 6:1-2; Colossians 3:16). Rather, Paul is teaching us to counterbalance our natural tendency to focus only on what is bad in those who oppose us. As you regain a more balanced view of the other person, you will often find it easier to overlook minor offenses or confront in a more loving, gentle, and productive manner.

❺   Practice what you have learned (v 9).

Paul's final instruction to Euodia and Syntyche (and to us) is both straightforward and encouraging.

What does Paul say will be the result of such faithfulness?

"The God of peace will be with you."

Facilitator's Guide: *Peacemaking*, Turning Point, P. O. Box 22127, Chattanooga, TN 37422-2127

There are many conflicts that can be properly resolved only through confrontation, confession, forgiveness, and cooperative negotiation; but there are hundreds more that can be properly resolved simply by overlooking minor offenses or relinquishing rights for the sake of God's kingdom. Therefore, before focusing on your rights, take a careful look at your responsibilities and before you go to remove the speck from your brother's eye, ask yourself, "Is this really worth fighting over?"

If you are presently involved in a conflict, these questions will help you to apply the principles presented in this session.

❶   Define the material issues in this conflict.

❷   Define the personal issues in this conflict.

❸   Which personal issues are having the greatest influence on you? On your opponent?

❹   Check your attitude:

a. Why can you "rejoice in the Lord" in this situation?

b. Have you been irritable, rude, or abrasive in this situation? How could your gentleness be more "evident" to others?

c. What have you been worried or anxious about? What would you like God to do for you or accomplish through this conflict?

d. What is good about the person with whom you are in conflict? What is right about his or her concerns? Do you have any good memories of your relationship? How has God helped you through that person?

As time permits, ask for volunteers to share one or more of the questions. Also include the prayer.

❺ Go on record with the Lord by writing a prayer based on the principles taught in this session.

In the prayer, answer these two questions.
- What offenses can you simply overlook?
- Which of the material issues can you give in on?

Additional Scripture References

Psalm 18	*Proverbs 20:3*	*1Corinthians 9:3-15*
Psalm 73:21-22	*Proverbs 26:17*	*Ephesians 4:2*
Proverbs 10:12	*Nehemiah 9:5-37*	*Philippians 2:5-11*
Proverbs 11:27	*Micah 6:8*	
Proverbs 15:18	*Luke 12:13-15*	

Closing Prayer

Ask God to provide each person with the wisdom needed as they go forward as peacemakers. Pray that each one will truly know the answer to the question: ***Is this really worth fighting over?***

Session **5** *Examine Yourself*

"Let us examine our ways and test them, and let us return to the LORD" (Lamentations 3:40).

Introduction

Allow 10 Minutes

Opening Prayer

Thank God for each person present. Thank Him for their desire to be peacemakers. Ask Him to be the guide for the group session.

Sharing Questions

As we are open to the Holy Spirit for personal examination, how does that increase our self-awareness?

We become aware and alert to our strengths (which can encourage us) and to our weaknesses (which can prevent and/or overcome life-impacting situations).

Self-Awareness

Allow 20-25 Minutes

The following story illustrates the importance of personal examination.

Read Chapter 5 from *The Peacemaker* for further preparation for this session.

Ask for a volunteer to read the opening story.

> *After many years of marriage, I can think of only one time I may have been entirely innocent of wrongdoing when my wife and I had an argument (and I am probably mistaken about that incident). Every other time we experienced a conflict, I either caused it or made it worse through sinful words or actions. Of course, when I am embroiled in the heat of battle, the last thing I naturally think about is my sin. However, after the smoke clears, I can always see something I should have done differently. With God's help, I am trying to speed up this process so I can avoid sinful reactions more often or at least face up to them more quickly.*
>
> *Because most of us do not like to admit we have sinned, we tend to conceal, deny, or rationalize our wrongs. If we cannot completely cover up what we have done, we try to minimize our wrongdoing by saying we simply made a "mistake" or an "error in judgment." Another way to avoid responsibility for our sins is to shift the blame to others or to say they made us act the way we did. When our wrongs are too obvious to ignore, it is easy to practice what I*

call the 40/60 Rule. It goes something like this: "Well, I know I'm not perfect, and I admit I am partially to blame for this problem. I'd say about 40 percent of the fault is mine. That means 60 percent of the fault is hers. Since she is 20 percent more to blame than I am, she should be the one to ask for forgiveness." I never actually say or think these exact words, but I sometimes catch myself using this general concept in subtle ways. By believing that my sins have been more than canceled by another's sins, I can divert attention from what I have done and avoid the call to repentance and confession. "If there is any confessing that needs to be done," I convince myself, "it needs to start with her."

Describe a situation where you practiced the 40/60 Rule.

Personal response.

Literally speaking, to sin means "to miss the mark." Sin is not an action against an impersonal set of rules. Rather, it is rebellion against God's personal desires and requirements.

In fact, we can sin against God by omission—by doing nothing. As James 4:17 tells us, "Anyone, then, who knows the good he ought to do and doesn't do it, sins." Therefore, if we are involved in a conflict and neglect opportunities to serve others (through gentle responses, loving confrontation, etc.), we are guilty of sin in God's eyes.

Spiritual Awareness Lead-In

1 John 1:8 indicates, "If we claim to be without sin, we deceive ourselves and the truth is not in us." Whenever we refuse to face up to our sins, we will eventually pay an unpleasant price. This is what King David discovered when he did not immediately repent of his sins. Psalm 32:3-5 describes the guilty conscience, emotional turmoil, and even the physical side effects he experienced until he confessed his sins to God.

Ask for a volunteer to read Psalm 32:3-5.

"When I kept silent, my bones wasted away through my groaning all day long. For day and night your hand was heavy upon me; my strength was sapped as in the heat of summer. Then I acknowledged my sin to you and did not cover up my iniquity. I said, 'I will confess my sins to the LORD'—and you forgave the guilt of my sin."

If it is difficult for you to identify and confess your wrongs, there are two things you can do. First, you can ask God to help you to see your sin clearly and repent of it regardless of what others may do. (See Psalm 139:23-24.)

Second, it is often helpful to ask for the candid insights and advice of a spiritually mature friend. (See Proverbs 12:15, 19:20.)

Facilitator's Guide: *Peacemaking*, Turning Point, P. O. Box 22127, Chattanooga, TN 37422-2127

Self-examination for the purpose of uncovering sinful habits and attitudes is never easy. Scripture provides the guidance we need.

Control Your Tongue

Before we can confess and renounce our sins, we must identify them. It is often wise to begin this process by examining what we have been saying to and about our opponents.

James 3:5-6
"The tongue is a small part of the body, but it makes great boasts" (v 5).
Describe the comparison to a great forest.

"A great forest is set on fire by a small spark" (v 5). Likewise the tongue "corrupts the whole person" (v 6).

Sinful speech takes many forms.

- **Reckless words**

Proverbs 13:3
To guard our lips is to guard our life.
What happens to those who speak rashly?

They "will come to ruin."

- **Grumbling and complaining**

Philippians 2:14-15
The Apostle Paul leaves no room for complaining.
Why do you think this is so important?

"So that you may become blameless and pure, children of God without fault in a crooked and depraved generation" (v 15).

Because negative and critical talk irritates, offends, and depresses other people which often leads them to begin grumbling and complaining as well.

- **Falsehood**

2 Corinthians 4:2
Falsehood involves more than outright lies; it includes any form of misrepresentation or deceit.
What did Paul recommend to replace secret and shameful ways and deception?

To set "forth the truth plainly."

- **Gossip**

Proverbs 16:28
Gossip is often both the spark and the fuel for conflict.
What does gossip do to friendships?

It "separates close friends."

To gossip means to reveal or discuss personal facts about another person for no legitimate purpose; it often betrays a confidence.

- **Slander**

2 Timothy 3:3-5

Slander involves speaking false and malicious words about another person.

What should we do when a slanderous person refuses to repent?

"Have nothing to do with them" (v 5).

People who generally refrain from reckless words, falsehood, gossip, and slander may still be guilty of **worthless talk** which can also contribute to conflict even if they intend no harm.

Heed Your Responsibilities

Our country has become so preoccupied with rights that many people give little thought to their responsibilities. There are three responsibilities in particular that seem to be increasingly ignored in our society.

- **Keep Your Word**

A great deal of conflict is the direct result of someone's failure to keep a commitment whether it was expressed in a contract, a marriage vow, an oath to God, or by a simple yes or no (Matthew 5:33-37).

Psalm 15:4

What importance does David place on the keeping of oaths?

We are to keep an oath "even when it hurts."

- **Respect Authority**

Another common source of conflict is the abuse of or rebellion against the authority God has established in the church, the government, the family, and the workplace. All legitimate authority has been established by God primarily for the purpose of maintaining peace and order (Romans 13:1-7).

God calls us to respect the positions of those in authority even when their personalities leave much to be desired. (See Matthew 23:1-3.)

Give an example.

Personal response.

Apply the Golden Rule

One of the most effective ways to determine your responsibilities and thereby discover whether or not you have sinned is to refer to the principle set forth in Matthew 7:12: "So in everything, do to others what you would have them do to you."

   Facilitator's Guide: *Peacemaking*, Turning Point, P. O. Box 22127, Chattanooga, TN 37422-2127

Acknowledge Wrongful Motives

James 4:1-3
Sinful words and actions common to conflict are merely symptoms of deeper problems.

According to verse 3, what is the root issue?

Ask with wrong [selfish] motives.

Matthew 15:19
From where do sinful thoughts, words, and actions come?

"Out of the heart."

The word heart is used in the Bible to describe more than just feelings. It often refers to our whole inner life, including thoughts and attitudes (Hebrews 4:12). Thus, when the Bible talks about changing our heart, it is calling for changes in feelings, desires, beliefs, expectations, thoughts, and attitudes. A supernatural transformation of your heart takes place when you accept Christ as your Savior, and then God works in you to continue the process of change. God promises: "I will cleanse you from all your impurities and from all your idols. I will give you a new heart and put a new spirit in you; I will remove from you your heart of stone and give you a heart of flesh" (Ezekiel 36:25b-26; cf. Hebrews 8:10).

Application

Allow 20 Minutes

Whenever you are involved in a conflict, it is important to consider if you may be contributing to the problem, either directly or indirectly. In some cases, you may have caused the controversy. In others, you may have aggravated a dispute by failing to respond to another person in a godly way. Therefore, before focusing on what others have done wrong, it is wise to carefully examine the way you have been thinking, speaking, and acting. In particular, you should try to identify the desires and motives (idols) that are leading you to behave in a sinful manner. With God's help, you can see where your ways do not line up with His purposes. That realization is the first step toward repentance which opens the way for confession, personal change, and the restoration of genuine peace.

As time permits, ask for volunteers to share one or more of the questions. Also, include the prayer.

If you are presently involved in a conflict, these questions will help you to apply the principles presented in this session.

❶ As you have talked to and about others in a conflict situation, have you been guilty of any of the following kinds of speech? If so, describe what you said.

- ❏ Reckless words
- ❏ Grumbling and complaining
- ❏ Falsehood
- ❏ Gossip
- ❏ Slander
- ❏ Worthless talk
- ❏ Hurtful or destructive words

❷ Are you guilty of any of the following sins? If so, describe what you did or failed to do.

- ❏ Uncontrolled anger
- ❏ Bitterness
- ❏ Evil or malicious thoughts
- ❏ Sexual immorality
- ❏ Laziness
- ❏ Defensiveness
- ❏ Self-justification
- ❏ Resistance to godly advice
- ❏ Greed
- ❏ Deficient work
- ❏ Withholding mercy and forgiveness
- ❏ Compulsive behavior
- ❏ Breaking your word
- ❏ Misusing authority
- ❏ Rebelling against authority

❸ Have you failed to respond to opportunities to do good to others in a conflict situation? How?

Facilitator's Guide: *Peacemaking*, Turning Point, P. O. Box 22127, Chattanooga, TN 37422-2127

❹ Go on record with the Lord by writing a prayer based on the principles taught in this session.

Additional Scripture References

Genesis 39:9	*Proverbs 28:13*	*Ephesians 5:21-24*
Numbers 5:6-7	*Proverbs 29:20*	*2 Timothy 2:16*
Leviticus 19:16	*Zechariah 3:1*	*James 2:10-11*
Psalm 36:2	*Matthew 5:33-37*	*James 5:9*
Psalm 51:3-4	*John 8:44*	*1 Peter 2:19-23*
Proverbs 17:28	*Acts 4:18-19*	*1 John 3:4*
Proverbs 21:23	*Romans 14:9*	
Proverbs 24:28	*Ephesians 4:29*	

Closing Prayer

Thank our Heavenly Father for setting before us the truth that will help us change to become more like His Son. Pray for the strength through the power of the Holy Spirit to acknowledge our sin, turn from our sinful ways, and live holy lives before Him.

Free Yourself from Sin

"He who conceals his sins does not prosper, but whoever confesses and renounces them finds mercy" (Proverbs 28:13).

Introduction

Allow 10 Minutes

Opening Prayer

Thank God for each person present. Thank Him for their commitment and faithfulness. Thank Him for the progress of the group.

Sharing Questions

When do you struggle with yourself and win, or when do you struggle with yourself and lose?

Personal response.

Self-Awareness

Allow 20-25 Minutes

God has provided a way to obtain forgiveness, clean up the past, and change undesirable habits. This process involves three basic steps: repentance, confession, and personal change.

Read Chapter 6 from *The Peacemaker* for further preparation for this session.

Repentance Is More Than a Feeling

Repentance is the first step in gaining freedom from sin. Repentance does not simply mean feeling uncomfortable, nor does it involve a mere apology. It means to change the way you think. Sometimes described as coming to our senses (Luke 15:17), repentance is a renouncing of sin and a turning to God.

A person proves his repentance not merely through words but also through actions that reflect a change in thinking (Acts 26:20).

Facilitator's Guide: *Peacemaking*, Turning Point, P. O. Box 22127, Chattanooga, TN 37422-2127

The Seven A's of Confession

Confession, the second step in dealing with sin, is one of the most liberating acts in life. The Bible provides clear and specific guidelines for an effective confession. They are listed below as the Seven A's of confession.

❶ Address Everyone Involved

As a general rule, you should confess your sins to every person who has been directly affected by your wrongdoing. Since all sins offend God by violating His will, all sins should be first confessed to Him (see Psalm 32:5; 41:4). In fact, until you are reconciled to God through confession, you will have a very difficult time being reconciled to others.

Whether a sin should be confessed to other people as well as to God depends on whether it was a "heart sin" or a "social sin." Since a heart sin takes place only in your thoughts, it does not directly affect others and needs to be confessed only to God.

Heart sins often give rise to social sins that actually affect other people. Some social sins involve acts of commission such as slander, stealing, or lying. They may also involve acts of omission such as failing to help someone in need, ignoring a person, giving the cold shoulder, or withholding forgiveness. Social sins must be confessed to those who have been affected by them.

If your sins have wronged only one person, that person is the only one to whom you need to confess; but if several people have been hurt by your behavior, you should confess your sin to each one. It is usually wise to talk to each person privately.

Give an example of a heart sin and a social sin.

Personal response.

❷ Avoid If, But, and Maybe

The best way to ruin a confession is to use words that shift the blame to others or that appear to minimize or excuse your guilt. Notice how the following so-called confessions are diluted by the words in italics.

"*Maybe* I could have tried harder."
"*Possibly* I should have waited to hear your side of the story."
"*I guess* I was wrong when I said those critical things about you; *I only did it because you made me so angry.*"
"I shouldn't have lost my temper, *but I was tired.*"
"*If you hadn't* _____, then I wouldn't have done _____."

Facilitator's Guide: *Peacemaking,* Turning Point, P. O. Box 22127, Chattanooga, TN 37422-2127   Session 6 ❺❸

Give a personal example of one of the above diluted confessions.

❸ **Admit Specifically**

The more precise you are when making a confession, the more likely you are to receive a positive response. Specific admissions help to convince others that you are honestly facing up to what you have done which, in turn, makes it easier for them to forgive you.

Here are some examples:

"My critical comments have not only hurt you, but they have offended God as well. I have disobeyed His command not to slander others."

"I've finally realized that I have completely failed to be the kind of husband God wants me to be. In Ephesians, He says I should love you as Christ loved His church, but I haven't even come close to living up to that standard."

Can you add a personal example to this list? Describe.

❹ **Apologize**

If you want someone to respond positively to a confession, make it a point to apologize for what you have done. An apology is an expression of sorrow or regret for hurting another person's feelings or interests. To be most effective, it will show that you understand how the other person felt as a result of your words or actions. Here are two examples of how this can be done:

"You must have been terribly embarrassed when I said those things in front of everyone. I'm very sorry I did that to you."

"I can see why you were frustrated when I didn't deliver the parts on time. I'm sorry I failed to keep my commitment to you."

Although you should not dwell excessively on feelings, it is important to show that you understand how other people feel and to express genuine regret for hurting them.

❺ **Accept the Consequences**

Sometimes it is helpful to accept the consequences of your actions. Otherwise, the person you have wronged may assume that you are simply trying to be released from your responsibilities. The prodigal son demonstrated this principle. After acknowledging that he had sinned against God and his father, he said, "I am no longer worthy to be called your son; make me like one of your hired men" (Luke 15:19).

  Facilitator's Guide: *Peacemaking*, Turning Point, P. O. Box 22127, Chattanooga, TN 37422-2127

Describe a situation where you accepted the consequences of your actions.

Personal response.

❻ Alter Your Behavior

Another way to demonstrate sincere repentance is to explain to the person you offended how you will alter your behavior in the future. A written plan for change often has practical benefits.

❼ Ask for Forgiveness and Allow Time

If you follow the six steps described above, many people will readily offer to forgive you. If the person to whom you have confessed does not express forgiveness, however, you may ask, "Will you please forgive me?" This question is a signal that you have done all that you can by way of confession and that the responsibility for the next move has shifted to the other person. This will often help the offended person to make and express the decision to forgive you. (The details of forgiveness will be discussed in Session 10.)

Spiritual Awareness Lead–In

Anytime we use a formula (like the Seven A's), we can turn it into a meaningless ritual and completely miss what God wants us to do.

What warning does Mark 7:5-13 offer?

Formulas can become merely traditions without proper focus. This usually happens when we start to use the formula for our own benefit instead of seeing it as a means to glorify God and serve other people.

The third step in dealing with sin is to work with God to change your future behavior. This requires renouncing sinful attitudes and conduct and turning away from *everything* that is contrary to God's will. This process fulfills the third opportunity of peacemaking; namely, becoming more Christ-like. We can change.

Meaningful change does not come about simply by *not* doing what is wrong. Real change is positive—it requires *replacing* our sinful behavior with godly habits (Ephesians 4:22-32). There are four basic ingredients of personal change.

Prayer
Prayer is the starting point for all meaningful change.

John 15:4-5
We cannot cultivate spiritual fruit apart from God's active assistance.

What does Jesus say about our personal accomplishments apart from Him?

"Apart from me you can do nothing" (v 5).

Psalm 139:23-24
Prayer is the means by which we seek that assistance.

What does David ask for in these verses?

For a heart that is pleasing to God.

Focus
Our focus must be on the Lord.

Colossians 3:1-2
We must consciously and deliberately focus on Christ.

How does the Apostle Paul emphasize this point?

"Set your hearts on things above . . . set your minds on things above" (Colossians 3:1-2).

1 Corinthians 10:14
Focusing on the Lord requires us to deal with idols.

What is an idol?

Anything that replaces God as the center of our loyalty, affection, or heart's desire.

What instructions does the Apostle Paul give?

"Flee from idolatry." Flee is a strong word. It means to escape by running away. This calls for deliberate, strenuous, and prolonged action.

How does one flee from an idol?

1. Through prayer, study of God's Word, and the counsel of mature Christian friends.
2. Confess your idolatry to God and ask for His help.
3. Set your affections and your thoughts on Christ.

Study
The Bible frequently emphasizes the close connection between transformed thinking and personal change.

Romans 12:1-2
In verse 2, Paul talks about being transformed by the renewing of your mind.

What does he say is necessary for this to happen?

"Do not conform any longer to the pattern of this world."

Ephesians 4:22-24
Paul encourages the Ephesians to live as children of light.

What does he say concerning the old self?

"Put off your old self, which is being corrupted by its deceitful desires" (v 22).

What does he say concerning attitude?

"To be made new in the attitude of your minds" (v 23).

Practice
Prayer, a new heart, and study prepare you for the final ingredient of personal change which is to "put on the new self" (Ephesians 4:24).

Philippians 4:9
We must put to practice what we are learning.

What is the promised result?

"And the God of peace will be with you."

Practice is not a casual process. Paul commanded Timothy to "pursue righteousness, faith, love and peace" (2 Timothy 2:22). Training is also the route to spiritual maturity (Hebrews 5:14).

Application

To be an effective peacemaker, deal honestly with your own faults. As Paul told Timothy, "If a man cleanses himself from [sin], he will be an instrument for noble purposes, made holy, useful to the Master and prepared to do any good work" (2 Timothy 2:21). This cleansing process takes place only through repentance, confession, and personal change. The more faithfully you pursue these steps, the more useful you will be to your Master. At the same time, after you get the log out of your own eye, you will be better prepared to help others.

If you are presently involved in a conflict, these questions will help you apply the principles presented in this session.

As time permits, ask for volunteers to share one or more of the questions. Also, include the prayer.

❶ As you look back at the way you have handled this conflict, do you see a need for repentance? Describe.

Personal response.

❷ Write an outline for your confession.
   a. *Address everyone involved.* To whom do you need to confess?
   b. *Avoid if, but, and maybe.* What excuses or blaming do you need to avoid?
   c. *Admit specifically.* What sins have you committed? What biblical principles have you violated?
   d. *Apologize.* How might others feel as a result of your sin?
   e. *Accept the consequences.* What consequences do you need to accept? How can you reverse the damage you have caused?
   f. *Alter your behavior.* What changes do you intend to make, with God's help, in the way you think, speak, and behave in the future?
   g. *Ask for forgiveness.* What might make the person whom you have wronged reluctant to forgive you? What can you do to make it easier for that person to forgive you?

❸ Go on record with the Lord by writing a prayer based on the principles taught in this session.

Additional Scripture References

Ezra 14:6	*Luke 15:21*	*Philippians 2:13*
Daniel 4:27	*Acts 3:19*	*1 Peter 1:8*
Matthew 6:21-34	*Galatians 5:22-23*	*1 Peter 1:15-16*
Matthew 7:9-11	*Ephesians 1:17-19*	*2 Peter 1:4-8*
Luke 6:36	*Ephesians 5:1-2*	*1 John 2:6*
Luke 11:42	*Philippians 1:9-11*	

Closing Prayer

Pray that each person would glorify God by seeking His help to be humble, confessing wrongs to one another, and coming to know God's peace.

Part III

Go and Show Your Brother His Fault

**If your brother sins against you,
go and show him his fault,
just between the two of you.
If he listens to you,
you have won your brother over.**
Matthew 18:15

---

from **The Peacemaker's Pledge**

Go and show your brother his fault — Instead of pretending that conflict doesn't exist or talking about others behind their backs, we will choose to overlook minor offenses, or we will talk directly and graciously with those whose offenses seem too serious to overlook. When a conflict with another Christian cannot be resolved in private, we will ask others in the body of Christ to help us settle the matter in a biblical manner.

Session 7 Restore the Sinner Gently

"Brothers, if someone is caught in a sin, you who are spiritual should restore him gently" (Galatians 6:1).

Introduction

Allow 10 Minutes

Opening Prayer

Thank God for each person present. Pray for His wisdom and direction for this group session.

Sharing Question

Who has had the most positive influence in your life as a peacemaker?

Personal response.

Self-Awareness

Allow 20–25 Minutes

As we saw in Session 1, conflict often presents opportunities to serve others. If we show genuine concern for the well-being of others and use our resources to help meet their needs, our Master will consider us to be "faithful and wise servants" (Matthew 24:45-51; cf. Luke 12:42-48). Therefore, even when we are in the midst of a conflict, we should be stewards on the lookout for ways to serve others.

Read Chapter 7 from *The Peacemaker* for further preparation for this session.

Describe some ways we can serve others in the midst of a conflict.

This can be done by helping others resolve material issues, by carrying burdens they are unable to bear, by introducing them to Christ, by teaching and encouraging, and by our example.

Facilitator's Guide: *Peacemaking*, Turning Point, P. O. Box 22127, Chattanooga, TN 37422-2127

We also need to be open to the opportunity to serve others by helping them learn where they have been wrong and need to change. Although many offenses can and should be overlooked, some problems are so serious they must be addressed or they will damage valuable relationships and result in unnecessary harm to other people. In this session we will consider several principles that will help you to decide whether an offense should be overlooked or confronted. In Session 8, we will examine the ingredients of a biblical confrontation. Then in Session 9, we will discuss what to do if a private confrontation does not resolve a problem.

Ask for a volunteer to read this story.

I recall one Sunday when I visited a small ranching community and preached a message on Matthew 5:21-24. After church, a friend took me out to lunch. Partway through our meal, a man I had seen in church that morning walked into the restaurant. Seeing me, he came over to our table smiling from ear to ear.

"I have to tell you what just happened," he said. "Your sermon really shook me up because I've got a neighbor who hasn't talked to me for two years. We had an argument about where to run a fence. When I wouldn't move it to where he thought it should be, he just turned his back on me and stomped away. Since I thought I was in the right, I've always figured it was up to him to make the first move at being friends again. This morning I saw that the Lord wants me to be the one to seek reconciliation, so right after church, I drove over to his house to talk with him. I told him I was sorry for being so stubborn two years ago and that I wanted to be friends again. He just about fell over. He said he felt badly all along for stomping away that day, but he didn't know how to come talk with me. Boy, was he glad I came to talk with him!"

If you learn someone has something against you, God wants you to take the initiative in seeking peace—even if you do not believe you have done anything wrong. If you believe that another person's complaints against you are unfounded or that the misunderstanding is entirely the other person's fault, you may naturally conclude you have no responsibility to take the initiative in restoring peace. This is a common but false conclusion for it is contrary to Jesus' specific teaching in Matthew 5:23-24.

Why is this a false conclusion?

"You have heard that it was said to the people long ago, 'Do not murder, and anyone who murders will be subject to judgment.' But I tell you that anyone who is angry with his brother will be subject to judgment. Again, anyone who says to his brother, 'Raca,' is answerable to the Sanhedrin. But anyone who says, 'You fool!' will be in danger of the fire of hell.

"Therefore, if you are offering your gift at the altar and there remember that your brother has something against you, leave your gift there in the front of the altar. First go and be reconciled to your brother; then come and offer your gift" (Matthew 5:21-24).

This command is not limited to situations where the other person has something justifiable against you. Jesus said to be reconciled if your brother has something against you implying that the obligation exists whether or not you believe his complaint is legitimate.

Spiritual Awareness Lead–In

Seeking peace with an alienated brother or sister enhances your Christian witness especially if he or she is the one who has done the wrong. (See Luke 6:32-36.)

In doing this, how do we model our heavenly Father?

By being merciful (v 36).

Spiritual-Awareness

Allow 20–25 Minutes

Another time you should go and talk to someone about a conflict is when that person's sins are too serious to overlook. This is why Jesus said, "If your brother sins, rebuke him, and if he repents, forgive him" (Luke 17:3). It is sometimes difficult to decide whether a sin is serious enough to call for confrontation.

Below are a few situations that may warrant this kind of attention along with biblical principles for dealing with them.

Is It Dishonoring God?
Sin is too serious to overlook if it is likely to bring significant dishonor to God.

Matthew 21:12-13
Jesus dealt with a situation in the temple area that was bringing dishonor to God's temple.

What was the basis for Jesus making this determination?

God's Word. " 'It is written,' he said to them, 'My house will be called a house of prayer,' but you are making it a den of robbers' " (v 13).

Romans 2:23-24
The Jews were guilty of dishonoring God.

How did they dishonor God?

They were hypocritical.

"You who brag about the law, do you dishonor God by breaking the law" (v 23)?

Is It Damaging Your Relationship?

As a general rule, you should not overlook an offense that has significantly damaged your relationship with another person.

Psalm 133:1
Anything that has disrupted the peace and unity between two Christians must be talked over and made right.

How does David describe the fruitfulness of brothers living "together in unity?"

As "good and pleasant."

Ephesians 4:3
Paul describes the effort we should make in keeping "the unity of the Spirit."

What kind of effort does he call for?

"Make every effort."

Is It Hurting Others?

An offense or disagreement is also too serious to overlook when it results in significant harm to you or others.

1 Corinthians 5:1-13
Paul commands Christians to confront serious and open sin quickly and firmly to save other believers from being led astray.

What sin is he referring to in this passage?

"Sexual immorality" (v 1).

What illustration does he use to show that sin can spread if not addressed?

"A little yeast works through the whole batch of dough" (v 6).

An offense can also adversely affect others if it is made public and other Christians take sides. When the peace and unity of the church are threatened in this way, the underlying problem needs to be addressed before it causes serious division (Titus 3:10).

Is It Hurting the Offender?

Sin needs to be confronted when it is seriously harming the offender, either by direct damage or by impaired relationship with God or other people.

Leviticus 19:17
This verse tells us to rebuke our sinful neighbor.

Why is this kind of rebuke needed?

"So you will not share in his guilt."

James 5:19-20
We are to bring back those who are wandering "from the truth."

What happens when we turn "a sinner from the error of his way"?

We "will save him from death and cover over a multitude of sins."

1 Timothy 5:13
The Bible endorses constructive confrontation, but that is not a license to be a busybody.

This verses warns against the "habit of being idle."

What does this kind of idleness develop into?

"Gossips and busybodies."

A Christian's responsibility to help others deal with serious sins can be understood more clearly by studying two particular words used in Galatians 6:1. In this passage, Paul told the Galatians to restore a brother who is "caught in a sin." The Greek word that is translated as "caught" (*prolambano*) means to be overtaken or surprised. Thus, the brother who needs our help is one who has been ensnared by a trespass when he was off guard.

It also helps to understand what Paul told the Galatians to do with a brother caught in sin. Instead of ignoring him or throwing him out, the Galatians were instructed to "restore him gently." The word translated as "restore" (*katartizo*) means to mend, repair, equip, complete, or prepare. This word is used several times in the New Testament to describe fishermen mending and preparing their nets (Matthew 4:21).

 **Application**

Allow 20 Minutes

Although it is often best simply to overlook the sins of others, there will be times when doing so only prolongs alienation and encourages them to continue acting in a hurtful manner. If you know someone has something against you, go to that person and talk about it even before you worship God. Moreover, if another person's sins are dishonoring God, damaging your relationship, hurting others, or hurting that person, one of the most helpful things you can do is to lovingly show that sinner where there is a need for change. With God's help and the right words (including your own confession), such a conversation will often lead to restored peace and stronger relationships.

If you are presently involved in a conflict, these questions will help you to apply the principles presented in this session.

As time permits, ask for volunteers to share one or more of the questions. Also, include the prayer.

Facilitator's Guide: *Peacemaking,* Turning Point, P. O. Box 22127, Chattanooga, TN 37422-2127

❶ Do you have any reason to believe that someone else has something against you? If so, why?

❷ How has the other person sinned in this situation?

❸ Would it be better to overlook the offense against you or to go and talk with the other person about it?

What would be the probable benefits and drawbacks of each course of action?

❹ Is the other person's sin too serious to overlook? More specifically:

Is it dishonoring God? How?

Is it damaging your relationship? How?

Is it hurting others? How?

Is it hurting that person? How?

Is it making that person less useful to the Lord?

➎ Which of the other person's sins do you need to confront?

➏ Do you need to confess any of your sins before you can confront the other person? If so, what will you do if the other person does not freely confess the sins?

➐ Go on record with the Lord by writing a prayer based on the principles taught in this session.

Additional Scripture References

2 Samuel 12:1-13	Isaiah 59:1-2	1 Timothy 5:19-20
Psalm 32:1-5	Romans 12:18	2 Timothy 4:2-4
Proverbs 10:17	Romans 14:13-19	Hebrews 13:21
Proverbs 24:11-12	Romans 15:14	1 Peter 1:6-7
Proverbs 27:5-6	Ephesians 4:30-31	

Closing Prayer

Ask for a volunteer to conclude the session in prayer.

 Facilitator's Guide: *Peacemaking*, Turning Point, P. O. Box 22127, Chattanooga, TN 37422-2127

Session 8 Speak the Truth in Love

"Speaking the truth in love, we will in all things grow up into him who is the Head, that is, Christ" (Ephesians 4:15).

Introduction

Allow 10 Minutes

Opening Prayer	Thank God for each person present. Thank Him for the faithfulness of each member of this group. Ask for the Holy Spirit's guidance as we look at ways to "speak the truth in love."
Sharing Question Did you ever get your mouth washed out with soap? Describe the language rules that were in your home as a child.	Personal response.

Self-Awareness

Allow 20–25 Minutes

Words play a key role in almost every conflict. When used properly, words promote understanding and encourage agreement. When misused, they usually aggravate offenses and drive people further apart. If your words seem to do more harm than good when it comes to resolving disagreements, do not give up. With God's help, you can improve your ability to communicate constructively.	Read Chapter 8 from *The Peacemaker* for further preparation for this session.

❶ *Speak Only to Build Up Others*

There are several types of words that cause or aggravate conflict. Therefore, if you want to be an effective peacemaker, make a conscious effort to avoid reckless words, falsehood (hearsay, speculation, exaggeration, partial truths), gossip, slander, and other forms of worthless talk. A good way to avoid these types of speech is simply to talk less about others.

Another way to avoid worthless talk is to get in the habit of talking *to* people with whom you are having a problem rather than *about* them. Check yourself whenever the tone of a conversation about a third party has become negative or critical.

Unless further discussion is likely to produce positive solutions to specific problems, it may be wise to end the conversation.

Describe a situation where you ended a negative conversation or where you should have concluded the discussion.

Personal response.

The best way to test your words is simply to ask yourself, "Is what I am saying or about to say likely to please and honor God?" If you can answer that question affirmatively, you can proceed with confidence.

❷   *Be Quick to Listen*

Good listening will enable you to gather more complete and accurate information which will improve your understanding of a problem and make possible more suitable solutions. Careful listening can send important messages that words alone often fail to communicate. It shows that you realize you do not have all of the answers, and it tells the other person that you value his or her thoughts and opinions.

When you are given undivided attention, what does that communicate to you?

It demonstrates genuine love and concern. It also shows sincerity and good faith.

❸   *Waiting*

One of the fundamental elements of effective listening is simply *waiting* patiently while others talk. Waiting is often difficult work, especially when you have limited time or strongly disagree with what others are saying; but unless you learn to wait as others talk, you will seldom get to the root of problems and may complicate matters with inappropriate reactions.

How may a jump to premature conclusions hinder effective communications?

We may miss much of what is being said and read into words intentions that are not actually there.

❹   *Attending*

The human mind can think at least four times faster than a person can talk. Therefore, even when you are listening to someone, your mind is often searching for something more to do. If you allow your mind to wander, you may miss much of what others are saying. Moreover, others can usually tell when you are distracted which discourages them in their efforts to communicate.

Facilitator's Guide: *Peacemaking*, Turning Point, P. O. Box 22127, Chattanooga, TN 37422-2127

❺ *Clarifying*

The purpose of clarifying is to make sure you understand what the other person is thinking. Here are some examples:
"Are you saying . . . ?"
"Let me see if I understand . . ."
"Tell me more about . . ."

❻ *Reflecting*

Reflecting or paraphrasing can summarize the other person's main points in your words and send them back in a constructive way. This shows you are listening and trying to understand.

❼ *Agreeing*

Ask yourself is there is any truth to what someone else is saying. If so, acknowledge your common ground before moving on to differences. These principles will produce controlled responses rather than emotional reactions. When you first agree with what you did wrong, your opponent is more likely to be willing to discuss how he or she has contributed to the problem.

❽ *Heal with Wise Communication*

• **CHOOSE THE RIGHT TIME AND PLACE**
Timing is an essential ingredient of effective confrontation. If possible, do not discuss sensitive matters with someone who is tired, worried about other things, or in a bad mood. Nor should you confront someone about an important concern unless you will have enough time to discuss the matter thoroughly.

• **BELIEVE THE BEST ABOUT OTHERS**
Believe the best about people until you have facts that prove otherwise. Confrontation is more likely to succeed if you avoid backing the person into a corner. Also, indicate that you are really open to hearing his or her side of the story.

• **TALK IN PERSON WHENEVER POSSIBLE**
As a general rule, communication is most effective if done face-to-face rather than by a telephone conversation because both people can see facial expressions and communicate with body language as well as with words.

• **PLAN YOUR WORDS**
The importance of planning your words when you know you must confront someone cannot be overemphasized. In delicate situations, careful planning can make the difference between restored peace or increased hostility.

- **Use "I" Statements**

"I" statements give information about yourself rather than attacking the other person—like when you make statements such as, "You are so insensitive," or "You are irresponsible."

An example of an "I" statement: "I feel _____; therefore, I need _____ ."

Example: "I feel <u>frustrated</u> when you commit to take out the trash and don't do it; therefore, I need <u>your help</u>."

- **Use the Bible Carefully**

It is often helpful, if not necessary, to refer to the Bible as a source of objective truth when you have a disagreement with another Christian. If this is not done with great care, however, it will alienate people rather than persuade them.

We should not quote the Bible to tear others down but to build them up in the Lord.

- **Recognize Your Limits**

Finally, whenever you must confront someone, remember there are limits to what you can accomplish. You can raise concerns, suggest solutions, and encourage reasonable thinking; but you cannot force change. God may use you as a spokesperson to bring certain issues to the attention of another person, but only God can actually penetrate the other person's heart and bring about repentance.

Spiritual Awareness Lead–In

Ephesians 4:15 is a passage that will guide us and filter our words for effective communication whether with enemies or friends.

What are Paul's instructions in this passage, and what will be the end results?

"Speaking the truth in love."

"We will in all things grow up into him who is the Head, that is, Christ."

Spiritual-Awareness

Allow 20–25 Minutes

There are a number of scriptures that underline the communication skills we have discussed. Here are some of those passages.

Facilitator's Guide: *Peacemaking*, Turning Point, P. O. Box 22127, Chattanooga, TN 37422-2127

Speak Only to Build Up Others

Proverbs 10:19
This verse talks to us about excessive words.

What happens when "words are many"?

"Sin is not absent."

Proverbs 25:15
This verse describes the value of patience.

Why is this important?

Through patience, a person can be persuaded.

Ephesians 4:29
This verse speaks to the need of building up others.

What does it say?

"Do not let any unwholesome talk come out of your mouths, but only what is helpful for building others up."

Be Quick to Listen

James 1:19
James gave this warning to the early church.

How does he tell us to listen?

"Be quick to listen, slow to speak and slow to become angry."

Proverbs 18:13
Waiting is a fundamental element of effective listening.

Describe the instructions given in this verse.

"He who answers before listening— that is his folly and his shame."

Heal with Wise Communication

Proverbs 12:18
Resolving conflict involves the ability to confront others in a clear, constructive, and persuasive manner.

Describe the instructions this verse provides.

"Reckless words pierce like a sword, but the tongue of the wise brings healing."

1 Corinthians 13:7
We are to *believe the best* about people.

What does this verse say about love?

Love always trusts.

Proverbs 14:22
The discipline of *planning* is highly commended in Scripture.

What is the benefit of those who plan what is good?

They "find love and faithfulness."

Proverbs 15:1
This verse tells us how to give answers.

How should we respond to angry reaction?

"A gentle answer turns away wrath."

We must recognize our limits. We should be concerned with faithfulness, not results. If you speak the truth in love and do all you can to confront the other person effectively, you will have succeeded in God's eyes regardless of how others respond. (See Acts 20:26-27.) God will take it from there—in His time, your words will produce exactly the results He wants.

Application

Allow 20 Minutes

Ron Kraybill, a respected Christian mediator, has noted that "effective confrontation is like a graceful dance from supportiveness to assertiveness and back again" (p. 7). This dance may feel awkward at first for those who are just learning it, but perseverance pays off. With God's help, you can learn to speak the truth in love by saying only what will build others up, listening responsibly to what others say, and using principles of wisdom. As you practice these skills and make them a normal part of your everyday conversations, you will be well-prepared to use them when conflict occurs. In developing the skills of loving confrontation, you can see for yourself that "the tongue of the wise brings healing" (Proverbs 12:18).

If you are presently involved in a conflict, these questions will help you to apply the principles presented in this session.

As time permits, ask for volunteers to share one or more of the questions. Also, include the prayer.

❶   When you talk to or about your opponent, what might you be tempted to say that would be harmful or worthless?

❷   How can you bless or build up your opponent with your words?

Facilitator's Guide: *Peacemaking*, Turning Point, P. O. Box 22127, Chattanooga, TN 37422-2127

❸ Which listening skill do you have a hard time with: waiting, attending, clarifying, reflecting, or agreeing?

❹ What is the best time and place to talk with your opponent?

❺ How can you demonstrate to your opponent that you believe the best about him or her?

❻ Write a brief summary of what you need to say or avoid saying, including:

- The issues that you believe should be addressed.
- Words and topics to avoid.
- Words that describe your feelings.
- A description of the effect the dispute is having on you and others.
- Your suggestions and preferences for a solution.
- The benefits that will be produced by cooperating to find a solution.

❼ How can you refer to Scripture in a helpful manner?

❽ Go on record with the Lord by writing a prayer based on the eight principles taught in this session.

Additional Scripture References

Psalm 141:5	Proverbs 15:31	Romans 12:14
Proverbs 10:10	Proverbs 17:10	1 Corinthians 4:12-13
Proverbs 11:12	Luke 6:27-28	1 Peter 3:9
Proverbs 15:5	Luke 23:34	
Proverbs 15:28	Acts 7:59-60	

Closing Prayer

Pray that each person will be an instrument of peace and unity and persevere in the development of loving confrontation skills. Ask God to give each person the heart and attitude of a servant.

Facilitator's Guide: *Peacemaking*, Turning Point, P. O. Box 22127, Chattanooga, TN 37422-2127

Session 9 Take One or Two Others Along

"But if he will not listen, take one or two others along, so that 'every matter may be established by the testimony of two or three witnesses' " (Matthew 18:16).

Introduction

Allow 10 Minutes

Opening Prayer

Thank God for each person present and each individual's desire to be a peacemaker. Thank God for His presence and concern for each group member.

Sharing Question

What is one thing that is happening in your life right now, and what makes it good?

Personal response.

Self-Awareness

Allow 20–25 Minutes

If you follow the peacemaking principles set forth in Scripture, you should be able to resolve most conflicts by talking in private with your opponent. However, when peace is not restored through personal peacemaking, it may be appropriate to involve one or more respected friends, church leaders, or other neutral individuals who can help to restore peace.

Read Chapter 9 from *The Peacemaker* for further preparation for this session.

The Resolution Process

STEP ONE: OVERLOOK MINOR OFFENSES

Before we talk about involving others in a conflict, it is wise to review the steps you should take to resolve a dispute in private. To begin with, you should carefully evaluate how you can use the situation as an opportunity to glorify God, serve others, and grow to be like Christ. Then you should seriously consider resolving the dispute unilaterally by overlooking minor offenses and giving up certain personal rights.

STEP TWO: TALK IN PRIVATE

If you need to confess a sin, if the other person's sin is too serious to overlook, or if the material issues are too significant to walk away from, you should go to the other person and seek to resolve the matter through discussion and negotiation.

What do you think would be the purpose in such a meeting?

If repeated efforts to resolve the matter in private fail and if the matter is too serious to overlook, you may then ask one or more other people to intervene.

STEP THREE: TAKE ONE OR TWO OTHERS ALONG

If a dispute cannot be resolved in private, then the biblical method is to involve one or two others. There are two ways outside people can become involved in a dispute.

By mutual agreement. If you and your opponent cannot resolve a dispute in private, you can suggest the two of you ask one or more neutral persons to meet with you in an effort to facilitate more productive dialogue. These neutral persons may be mutual friends, church leaders, respected individuals in your community, or even trained peacemakers such as you would find through the Institute for Christian Conciliation (a division of Peacemaker® Ministries). For the purposes of this discussion, these persons will be referred to as "conciliators."

Conciliators do not have to be professionally trained to be of service to you. Rather, they should be wise and spiritually mature Christians who are worthy of your respect and trust.

On your own initiative. While mutual agreement is always preferable, it is not actually required if your opponent professes to be a Christian. Matthew 18:16 indicates you may seek help from conciliators even if your opponent does not want it. Before you take this step, however, it is wise and often beneficial to warn your opponent what you are about to do.

What might you say in such a situation?

To win others over—not to win over others.

Example: "Bob, I would prefer to resolve this matter just between the two of us. Since that has not happened and because this involves issues that are too important to walk away from, my only other option is to obey what the Bible commands which means asking some people from our churches to help us out. I would prefer that we go together to get that help, but if you will not cooperate, I'll ask for it by myself."

Facilitator's Guide: *Peacemaking*, Turning Point, P. O. Box 22127, Chattanooga, TN 37422-2127

What do conciliators do? Conciliators can play a variety of roles in a conflict. Their primary role is to help you and your opponent make the decisions needed to restore peace. At first, they may simply facilitate communication by encouraging both sides to listen more carefully to each other. They may also help to determine the facts by listening carefully themselves, by asking appropriate questions, and by helping you and the other person obtain additional facts.

STEP FOUR: TELL IT TO THE CHURCH (CHURCH DISCIPLINE)

If your opponent professes to be a Christian and yet refuses to listen to the conciliators' counsel and if the matter is too serious to overlook, Jesus commands you to "tell it to the church" (Matthew 18:17). This does not mean standing up in a worship service and broadcasting the conflict to church members and visitors alike since unwarranted publicity is totally inconsistent with the tenor of Matthew 18. It does mean bringing the matter to the attention of church leaders and asking for them to exercise the spiritual authority given to the church.

Do you think there is ever a time when a Christian may properly disobey church discipline?

STEP FIVE: TREAT HIM AS A NONBELIEVER

The church has no power to decide whether a person *is* a believer. Instead, the church is called only to make a functional decision: If a person behaves like a nonbeliever would—namely, by disregarding the authority of Scripture and of Christ's church—he is to be treated as a nonbeliever.

Consider this analogy. When a patient has cancer, it is not easy for his doctor to tell him about it because it is a truth that is painful to hear and difficult to bear. Even so, any doctor who diagnoses cancer but fails to report it to a patient would be guilty of malpractice. After all, a patient can be properly treated only after the disease has been identified. Sin works in the same way. Left undiagnosed and untreated, it causes increasing grief and spiritual deterioration (Proverbs 10:17, 13:18, 29:1; Romans 6:23).

The only time a Christian may properly disobey his church is when its instructions are clearly contrary to what the Scriptures themselves teach. (See Matthew 23:1-3; Acts 4:18-20.)

Spiritual Awareness Lead–In

In 1 Corinthians 6:1-8, the Apostle Paul instructs Christians to resolve their legal disputes with the help of fellow Christians rather than in secular courts.

Why are secular courts not advisable?

> Because it is done "in front of unbelievers!" (v 6).
>
> It is a poor testimony to unbelievers.

If a person refuses to listen to the church, the church should obey Jesus' command to respond to this rebellion by treating the person as a nonbeliever. As a result, 1 Corinthians 6:1-6, which applies only to disputes between Christians, is no longer applicable to your situation. In other words, once you have exhausted your remedies through the church, you may treat your opponent like any other person. This means you may consider turning to the civil courts to resolve your conflict but only if your answer is "yes" to the question: "Would my Master be pleased and honored if I use my time and resources to pursue this matter in court?"

Spiritual-Awareness

Allow 20–25 Minutes

Below are some biblical principles that guide the resolution process when an offense cannot be overlooked.

Talk in Private

Matthew 18:15
When should one go privately to show a brother or sister his or her fault?

> When they sin against you. This principle would also apply to any disagreement or misunderstanding.

What happens if this person listens to you?

> "You have won your brother over."

Every effort should be made to communicate in a wise and loving manner.

Take One or Two Others Along

Matthew 18:16
If a dispute cannot be resolved in private, Jesus tells us to ask other people to get involved.

Why is this important?

> "So that 'every matter may be established by the testimony of two or three witnesses.' "

Galatians 6:1
We are encouraged to help people caught in sin.

What qualification is necessary in this verse for a conciliator?

> "You who are spiritual."

    Facilitator's Guide: *Peacemaking*, Turning Point, P. O. Box 22127, Chattanooga, TN 37422-2127

Tell It to the Church (Church Discipline)

Matthew 18:17
This verse holds the key to when the person should be disciplined by the church.

What is it?

"If he refuses to listen to them" (the one or two others who were involved in the previous step).

Treat Him As a Nonbeliever

Matthew 18:17
We are to deal with Christians who refuse to act justly, seek peace, and be reconciled with other Christians.

What are Jesus' instructions?

"Treat him as you would a pagan or a tax collector."

If a person behaves like a nonbeliever would—namely, by disregarding the authority of Scripture and of Christ's church— he is to be treated as a nonbeliever.

As in secular arbitration, the church's opinion is intended to be binding on its own member, whether the party likes it or not. As Matthew 18:18-20 teaches, the church speaks with the authority of Christ when it acts pursuant to its biblical mandate to deal with sin (Matthew 16:18; Hebrews 13:17).

Whose authority is the church exercising when it pronounces discipline?

God's authority.

It is important to emphasize that each step of this process must be done in Jesus' name (Matthew 18:20). Each step must be accompanied by diligent prayer; careful investigation; proper application of Scripture; a loving concern for other people; and above all else, a sincere desire to please and honor God. Most conflicts between Christians can be resolved simply by following the first two steps (Matthew 18:15-16). As Supreme Court Justices Burger and Scalia have indicated, civil judges would be more than happy to see Christians resolving their disputes in the church rather than in court. More importantly, such faithfulness honors God, promotes just settlements, and helps to preserve relationships that need not be lost.

If you are presently involved in a conflict and have not been able to resolve it privately, these questions will help you to apply the principles presented in this session.

As time permits, ask for volunteers to share one or more of the questions. Also, include the prayer.

❶ Are the personal or material issues in this conflict too serious to overlook or walk away from? Why?

❷ Why do you think your efforts to resolve this dispute in private have failed? Is there anything you could still do to resolve it in private?

❸ If you must seek outside help to resolve this dispute, are there any persons who would likely be trusted and respected both by you and your opponent?

❹ What will you say to your opponent to encourage him or her to allow other people to meet with the two of you to help resolve this dispute? In particular, how would you describe the advantages of getting outside assistance?

❺ If your opponent refuses to work voluntarily with others, would it be better to drop the matter or to ask the church to get involved? Why?

❻ If all other avenues have failed to resolve this matter and you are considering filing a lawsuit, have you satisfied these three conditions:

- Have you exhausted church remedies? How?

- Are the rights you are seeking to assert biblically legitimate? What makes you think so?

- Is there a righteous purpose for your lawsuit? In particular, what good will a lawsuit do for God? For your opponent? For you?

❼ Go on record with the Lord by writing a prayer based on the principles taught in this session.

Additional Scripture References

1 Samuel 16:7	*Acts 5:27-32*	*1 Corinthians 10:31-11:1*
Ezekiel 34:4	*Romans 13:1-7*	*2 Corinthians 2:5-11*
Ezekiel 34:8-10	*Romans 16:17*	*2 Thessalonians 3:14-15*
Mark 2:17	*1 Corinthians 5:9-11*	*Revelation 2:23*
John 4:1-18	*1 Corinthians 6:5*	

Closing Prayer

Thank God for loving us enough not to leave us alone in our sin. Thank Him for caring for us by clearly providing a process that seeks to restore and not simply to judge.

Facilitator's Guide: *Peacemaking*, Turning Point, P. O. Box 22127, Chattanooga, TN 37422-2127

Part IV

Go and Be Reconciled

First go and be reconciled to your brother; then come and offer your gift.

Matthew 5:24

from **The Peacemaker's Pledge**

Go and be reconciled — Instead of accepting premature compromise or allowing relationships to wither, we will actively pursue genuine peace and reconciliation—forgiving others as God, for Christ's sake, has forgiven us, and seeking just and mutually beneficial solutions to our differences.

Session 10 Forgive as God Forgave You

"Bear with each other and forgive whatever grievances you may have against one another. Forgive as the Lord forgave you" (Colossians 3:13).

Introduction

Allow 10 Minutes

Opening Prayer

Thank God not only for allowing us to know and fellowship with Him but also for the privilege of belonging to one another in a caring community of believers in Jesus Christ.

Sharing Question

How is the Holy Spirit speaking to you as a result of our bible study?

Personal response.

Self-Awareness

Allow 20–25 Minutes

Christians are the most forgiven people in the world; therefore, we should be the most forgiving people in the world. As most of us know from experience, however, it is often difficult to forgive others genuinely and completely. We often find ourselves practicing a form of forgiveness that is neither biblical nor healing.

Read Chapter 10 from *The Peacemaker* for further preparation for this session.

For example, sometimes people say, "I forgive him—I just don't want to have anything to do with him again."

Where would we be if this were the way the Lord forgave us?

Personal response.

Neither a Feeling nor Forgetting nor Excusing

To understand what forgiveness is, we must first see what it is not. First, forgiveness is not a feeling. It is an act of the will. Forgiveness involves a decision not to think or talk about what someone has done, and God calls us to make this decision regardless of our feelings.

Facilitator's Guide: *Peacemaking,* Turning Point, P. O. Box 22127, Chattanooga, TN 37422-2127

Second, forgiveness is not forgetting. Forgetting is a *passive* process in which a matter fades from memory merely with the passing of time. Forgiving is an *active* process; it involves a conscious choice and a deliberate course of action.

When God says He "remembers your sins no more" (Isaiah 43:25), He is not saying He *cannot* remember our sins. Rather, He is promising He *will not* remember them. When He forgives us, He chooses not to mention, recount, or think about our sins ever again. Similarly, when *we* forgive, we must consciously decide not to think or talk about what others have done to hurt us. This may require a lot of effort, especially when an offense is still fresh. Fortunately, when we decide to forgive someone and stop dwelling on an offense, painful memories usually begin to fade.

How have you dealt with the issue of forgiving and forgetting?

Personal response.

Forgiveness Is a Decision

A woman went to her pastor for advice on improving her marriage. When the pastor asked what her greatest complaint was, she replied, "Every time we get into a fight, my husband gets historical." When her pastor said, "You mean *hysterical*," she responded, "I mean exactly what I said. He keeps a mental record of everything I've done wrong; and whenever he's mad, I get a history lesson."

Having never learned the true meaning of forgiveness, many people destroy important relationships by keeping a record of the wrongs of others. At the same time, they deprive themselves of the peace and freedom that comes through genuine forgiveness.

Describe a situation where you made the decision to forgive.

Personal response.

Forgiveness may be described as a decision to make four promises:

❶ "I will not think about this incident."
❷ "I will not bring up this incident again and use it against you."
❸ "I will not talk to others about this incident."
❹ "I will not allow this incident to stand between us or hinder our personal relationship."

When Should You Forgive?

When an offense is too serious to overlook and the offender has not yet repented, you may need to approach forgiveness as a two-stage process. The first stage may be called *positional forgiveness* and the second *transactional forgiveness*. Positional forgiveness is unconditional and is a commitment you make to God (see Mark 11:25; Luke 6:28; Acts 7:60). You promise to strive to maintain a loving and merciful attitude toward someone who has offended you. It is a decision to make the first promise of forgiveness which means you will not dwell on the hurtful incident or seek vengeance or retribution in thought, word, or action. Instead, by God's grace, you will keep yourself in a "position of forgiveness" in which you pray for the other person and are ready to pursue complete reconciliation as soon as he or she repents.

Transactional forgiveness is conditional on the repentance of the offender and takes place between you and that person (Luke 17:3-5). It is a commitment to make the other three promises of forgiveness to the offender.

Have you experienced transactional forgiveness? Describe.

Personal response.

Both stages of forgiveness were vividly demonstrated by God. When Christ died on the cross, He took the position of forgiveness, maintaining an attitude of love and mercy toward those who put him to death. "Father, forgive them, for they do not know what they are doing" (Luke 23:34). At Pentecost, the Father's answer to Jesus' prayer was revealed. Three thousand people heard Peter's Pentecost message and were cut to the heart when they realized they had crucified the Son of God. As they repented of their sin, the transaction of forgiveness was completed, and they were fully reconciled to God (Acts 2:36-41). This is exactly the pattern you should follow: "Forgiving each other, just as in Christ God forgave you" (Ephesians 4:32).

Draw on God's Strength

Above all else, remember that true forgiveness depends on God's grace. If you try to forgive others on your own, you are in for a long and frustrating battle; but if you continually ask for and rely on God's strength, you can forgive even the most painful offenses. God gives us His grace through Scripture, through biblical counseling, and through the Holy Spirit. This grace was powerfully displayed in the life of Corrie ten Boom who had been imprisoned with her family by the Nazis for giving aid to Jews during World War II. Her father and sister, Betsie, died as a result of the brutal treatment they received in the concentration camps. Corrie survived and traveled throughout the world after the war testifying to God's love, even finding the strength in Christ to forgive her Nazis tormentors.

Spiritual Awareness Lead–In

To forgive someone means to release from liability to suffer punishment or penalty. *Aphiemi*, a Greek word that is often translated as "forgive," means to let go, release, or remit. It often refers to debts that have been paid or canceled in full (Matthew 6:12; 18:27, 32). *Charizomai*, another word for "forgive," means to bestow favor freely or unconditionally. This word shows that forgiveness is undeserved and cannot be earned (Luke 7:42-43; 2 Corinthians 2:7-10; Ephesians 4:32; Colossians 3:13).

How would you describe forgiveness as a gift?

It is something you give. It is something you receive.

piritual-Awareness

Allow 20–25 Minutes

The four promises of forgiveness tear down the wall that stands between you and a person who has wronged you. Forgiveness does not end there however. After you demolish an obstruction, you usually have to clear away some debris and do some repair work. The Bible calls this "reconciliation," a process involving a change of attitude that leads to a change in the relationship. More specifically, to be reconciled means to replace hostility and separation with peace and friendship. This is what Jesus had in mind when He said, "Go and be reconciled with your brother" (Matthew 5:24; cf. 1 Corinthians 7:11; 2 Corinthians 5:18-20). It means inviting a former opponent back into your life.

Unless you take definite steps to demonstrate your forgiveness, the other person may doubt your sincerity and withdraw from you. These problems can be significantly reduced if you pursue reconciliation at three different levels.

In Thought

Luke 6:27-28
We need God's help to get rid of painful thoughts and feelings.

What are the four instructions in this passage?	• "Love your enemies." • "Do good to those who hate you." • "Bless those who curse you." • "Pray for those who mistreat you."
When we replace negative thoughts and memories with biblical principles, we are practicing the *replacement principle*. *Philippians 4:8* This passage focuses on *right thinking*. How does this verse help us with the *replacement principle*?	By replacing negative thoughts and memories with positive ones.

In Word

2 Corinthians 2:7 The *replacement principle* applies to our words as well as our thoughts. How does this verse express verbal affirmation?	Paul commanded the church not only to forgive but also to comfort.
As you verbally reaffirm your friendship and sincerely build up the other person, both of you should experience improved attitudes and feelings.	

In Deed

1 John 3:18 To be reconciled to someone, apply the *replacement principle* to your actions as well. What should be the anchor of our actions according to this verse?	Truth.
C. S. Lewis noted, "Don't waste time bothering whether you 'love' your neighbor; act as if you did. As soon as we do this, we find one of the great secrets. When you are behaving as if you loved someone, you will presently come to love him" (p. 116).	

What About the Consequences?

2 Samuel 12:11-14 Forgiveness does not automatically release a wrongdoer from all the consequences of sin. Even though God forgave David for adultery and murder, God did not shield him from all the consequences that naturally flowed from his sin. What were the consequences of David's sin in verse 14?	"The son born to you will die."

Following God's example, you should remove any walls that stand between you and a repentant wrongdoer. It may also be appropriate to relieve that person from at least some of the consequences of his or her sin (Genesis 50:15-21; 2 Samuel 16:5-10, 19:18-23). For example, if someone negligently damaged your property and is truly unable to pay for needed repairs, you may decide to bear the cost yourself. Such mercy is especially appropriate when the offender is sincerely determined not to repeat that sin.

On the other hand, there may be times when you forgive someone but cannot afford to absorb the consequences of such wrongdoing. Or even if you could bear the cost, doing so may not be the wisest and most loving thing for an offender, especially one caught in a pattern of irresponsibility or misconduct. As Proverbs 19:19 warns, "A hot-tempered man must pay the penalty; if you rescue him, you will have to do it again."

Application

Allow 20 Minutes

This is what reconciliation is all about. By thought, word, and deed, you can demonstrate forgiveness and rebuild relationships with people who have offended you. No matter how painful the offense, with God's help, you can make four promises and imitate the forgiveness and reconciliation that was demonstrated on the cross. By the grace of God, you can forgive as the Lord forgave you.

If you are presently involved in a conflict and have not been able to resolve it privately, these questions will help you apply the principles presented in this session.

As time permits, ask for volunteers to share one or more of the questions. Also, include the prayer.

❶   How has your opponent sinned against you?

❷   Write out the four promises that you will make to your opponent at this time to indicate your forgiveness.

❸ If you are having a hard time forgiving your opponent:

- Is it because you are not sure he or she has repented? If so, how could you encourage confirmation of repentance?

- Do you think your opponent must somehow earn or deserve your forgiveness? Are you trying to punish by withholding forgiveness? Are you expecting a guarantee that the offense will not happen again? If you have any of these attitudes or expectations, what do you need to do?

- How did your sins contribute to this problem? Which of these sins will God refuse to forgive? How can you imitate His forgiveness?

- Read Matthew 18:21-35. What is the point of this passage? How does it apply to you?

- How might God be working for good in this situation?

- What has God forgiven you for in the past? How serious are your opponent's sins against you when compared to your sins against God? How can you show God that you appreciate His forgiveness?

❹ How can you demonstrate forgiveness or promote reconciliation:

In thought?

In word?

In deed?

❺ Go on record with the Lord by writing a prayer based on the principles taught in this session.

Facilitator's Guide: *Peacemaking*, Turning Point, P. O. Box 22127, Chattanooga, TN 37422-2127

Additional Scripture References

Psalm 32:1-5	*Isaiah 43:25*	*Ephesians 4:32*
Psalm 103:9-12	*Isaiah 53:4-6*	*1 Peter 2:24-25*
Psalm 130:3-4	*Jeremiah 31:34*	
Isaiah 6:1-5	*1 Corinthians 13:5*	

Closing Prayer

Thank God for forgiving our sins which separated us from Him. Thank Him for teaching us that we are to forgive others in the same manner He has forgiven us.

Session **11** *Look Also to the Interests of Others*

> *"Each of you should look not only to your own interests, but also to the interest of others" (Philippians 2:4).*

Introduction

Allow 10 Minutes

Opening Prayer	Ask for a volunteer to open in prayer and ask God's direction in this session. If no one volunteers, either you or your co-facilitator should do so.
Sharing Question What do you especially value about this group?	Personal response.

Self-Awareness

Allow 20–25 Minutes

Many people automatically resort to a competitive style when negotiating material issues thereby aggressively pursuing the results they desire and letting their opponents look out for themselves.

Although this approach may be appropriate when prompt results are needed or when someone is defending important moral principles, a competitive approach often fails to produce the best possible solution to a problem.

Cooperative negotiation may be described as a combination of love and wisdom. When you need to negotiate, P A U S E. This acronym stands for the following steps:

Prepare

Affirm relationships

Understand interests

Search for creative solutions

Evaluate options objectively and reasonably

Read Chapter 11 from *The Peacemaker* for further preparation for this session.

Facilitator's Guide: *Peacemaking*, Turning Point, P. O. Box 22127, Chattanooga, TN 37422-2127

Here is the situation we will consider throughout this session.

Jim and Julie Johnson live on a two-acre tract of land outside of town. Their nearest neighbors, Steve and Sally Smith, have similar acreage. The two houses are located within a hundred feet of each other on adjacent corners of the properties. The Smiths raise border collies as a hobby and a small business. A few weeks ago, they acquired a new dog named Molly who barks sporadically several evenings a week. The annoying barking has been keeping the Johnsons awake at night, and their children are complaining about being tired in school. To make matters worse, the Smiths recently began to exercise and feed Molly at 5 A.M. The resulting noise robs the Johnsons of another hour of sleep.

A week or so ago, Jim noticed Sally working in her garden, and he went over to ask if she would do something about the barking. She said she was sorry, and for a few days the barking subsided. Within a week, however, it started again and seemed even worse than before. Yesterday another neighbor told Julie that Steve had called everyone in the subdivision to see whether the dog was bothering them. In the process, he had said some very critical things about Jim.

Julie has conducted her own survey and found out that only a few of her neighbors have been annoyed by Molly's barking. Two neighbors are hard of hearing, and some of the others live in earth homes that block out most sounds. Julie then checked with the county attorney and found out that it is a misdemeanor to keep a dog that disturbs a "considerable number of persons" in a neighborhood. Unfortunately, the county attorney apparently does not believe the dog has disturbed enough people to justify misdemeanor charges. Therefore, Jim and Julie will need to negotiate a solution without the aid of the authorities.

Prepare

Remember, the purpose of any negotiation from God's standpoint is reconciliation (redemption). So plan your steps and work through the process with these three questions at the forefront:

1. How can we glorify God?
2. How can we serve others?
3. How can we grow to be like Christ?

Since the problem with the barking dog did not need to be resolved immediately, Jim and Julie took several days to prepare to negotiate with the Smiths. Each day they prayed for the Smiths and asked God for wisdom and discernment.

Jim and Julie also spent some time discussing what they would do if the Smiths refused to do anything about the barking. Although they were tempted to find a way to retaliate and make life difficult for the Smiths, they knew that would not please or honor God. Therefore, they decided that if they could not stop the barking right away, they would simply work harder at cultivating a positive relationship with the Smiths.

How would you suggest cultivation of a positive relationship with the Smiths?

Ask for a volunteer to read this story.

Personal response.

Affirm Relationships

A conflict generally involves two basic ingredients: people and a problem. All too often, we ignore the feelings and concerns of the people and focus all of our attention on the problems that separate us. One way to avoid these unnecessary complications is to affirm your respect and concern for your opponent throughout the negotiation process.

Affirming words must be backed up with comparable actions.

Why do you think affirming their relationship with the Smiths should be a basic step of the Johnsons' initial request for a meeting?

By asking for a meeting instead of demanding it, they conveyed courtesy and respect.

Understand Interests

It is important to understand that "interests" differ from "issues" and "positions."

An *issue* is an identifiable and concrete question that must be addressed. For example: "Should the Smiths do something to stop Molly's barking?"

A *position* is a desired outcome. For example: "If the dog keeps barking, you should get rid of her."

An *interest* is what motivates people. It is a concern, desire, need, limitation, or something a person values. For example: "I like breeding and training dogs," or "My kids need to sleep."

As Jim and Julie considered the Smiths' interest in keeping Molly, they realized that solving this problem was going to take some careful thinking.

Search for Creative Solutions

The fourth step in the PAUSE strategy is to search for solutions that will satisfy as many interests as possible. This process should begin with spontaneous inventing. Everyone should be encouraged to mention any idea that comes to mind. Imagination and creativity should be encouraged while evaluating and deciding should be postponed. As you are searching for possible solutions, avoid the assumption that there is only one answer to your problem.

Facilitator's Guide: *Peacemaking*, Turning Point, P. O. Box 22127, Chattanooga, TN 37422-2127

After discussing their interests, the Johnsons and the Smiths began to search for some creative solutions to their problems. Here are some of the ideas:

- Put a fence between the houses.
- Exercise the dogs a little later in the morning.
- Move the Johnson children's bedrooms to the far side of the house.

What other creative solutions can you think of?

Personal response.

Evaluate Options Objectively and Reasonably

When Jim and Julie met with the Smiths, they were prepared to offer some objective information and some creative proposals.

First, they showed Steve their journal indicating the relationship between Molly's barking and people passing by on the highway. Steve acknowledged that Molly was probably barking at those people, but he repeated his concerns about the lack of shade and his lack of time to move the kennel.

Jim said, "How about if I come over next Saturday and help you dismantle and move your kennel? I'll bet it would only take us three or four hours. As far as needing shade, my father-in-law has dozens of young trees on his land north of town. We could take your pickup truck out there and bring back all the trees you'd need to put in a great shelter belt around the kennel."

Jim's proposal was so reasonable that Steve could not find a way to say no. That is when Julie added her suggestion: "I have an idea about the problem of your going out of town. I talked with our daughter, Karen, and she said she would be delighted to take care of your dogs. Also, I should tell you that if you let her care for them, she would prefer not to be paid in cash. What she would really like is a puppy out of one of Molly's litters next year."

Once the conversation turned to puppies, Steve's heart really softened. The more he thought about the suggestions Jim and Julie were making, the more he liked them. It took a while to work out all of the details, but later conversations became even easier as the two families learned to cooperate more and more.

Spiritual Awareness Lead–In

Having a loving concern for others does not mean always giving in to their demands (Philippians 2:4). Jesus calls us to be "as shrewd as snakes and as innocent as doves" (Matthew 10:16).

What do you think it means to be "as shrewd as snakes?"

"The Greek word *phronimos*, translated 'shrewd' in this passage, means to be prudent, sensible, and practically wise" (Vine, p. 679).

Spiritual-Awareness

Allow 20–25 Minutes

Cooperative negotiation is highly commended by Scripture which repeatedly commands us to have an active concern for the needs and well-being of others.

Matthew 22:39
We are commanded to love our neighbor.

To whom are we to compare this love?

"As yourself."

Matthew 7:12
This verse "sums up the Law and the Prophets."

What is this summary?

"So in everything, do to others what you would have them do to you."

Proverbs 14:22
Preparation is one of the most important elements of successful negotiation.

What happens to those "who plan what is good?"

They find "love and faithfulness."

1 Samuel 25:1-44
David's popularity among the people of Israel had become so great that King Saul became jealous and tried to kill him. David and several hundred of his supporters fled into the desert where they lived as mercenaries. During this time, they protected the flocks and herds of the local inhabitants from marauders. One of the people who had benefited from David's protection was a wealthy landowner named Nabal. When David's provisions ran low, he sent ten young men to ask Nabal for food. In spite of the good David had done for him, Nabal denied the request and hurled insults at the young men. When David learned of this, he was furious. He immediately set out with four hundred armed men determined to kill Nabal and all of his men.

In the meantime, Nabal's wife, Abigail, learned what Nabal had done. Seeing the danger her husband was in, she set out to negotiate a peace treaty with David. First, she loaded a large amount of food on several donkeys and instructed her servants to take it to David. (Very wise preparation!) She then mounted her own donkey and set out to intercept him before he had time to launch his attack. When Abigail met David at the foot of the mountains, she dismounted and bowed down before him and said:

My lord, let the blame be on me alone. Please let your servant speak to you; hear what your servant has to say. . . . *(T)he LORD has kept you, my master, from bloodshed and from avenging yourself with your own hands* . . . Please forgive your servant's offense, for the LORD will certainly make a lasting dynasty for my master, because he fights the LORD's battles. *Let no wrongdoing be found in you as long as you live.* . . . When the LORD has done for my master every good thing he promised concerning him and has appointed him leader over Israel, *my master will not have on his conscience the staggering burden of needless bloodshed or of having avenged himself*" (vv 24-31, emphasis added).

Abigail clearly affirmed her concern and respect for David. More importantly, instead of lecturing him or talking directly about her own concerns, Abigail focused on David's primary interest in this situation.

What was that interest?

What was David's response to Abigail?

In being found righteous before God.

"Praise be to the LORD, the God of Israel, who has sent you today to meet me. May you be blessed for your good judgment and for keeping me from bloodshed this day and from avenging myself with my own hands" (vv 32-33).

David's rage had blinded him to his own interest, but Abigail's brilliant appeal brought him to his senses.

Daniel 1:11-16
This passage contains an outstanding example of an objective evaluation.

When Daniel learned that he and his companions would be provided with food and wine that was ceremonially unclean, he asked the chief official for permission to eat different food (v 8). Although the official was sympathetic, he refused Daniel's request saying, "I am afraid of my lord the king. . . . Why should he see you looking worse than the other young men your age? The king would then have my head because of you" (v 10). This left Daniel with some interesting choices. He could eat the food and defile himself, or he could refuse to eat and either starve to death or be killed for disobedience.

Daniel carefully prepared his negotiation strategy. He affirmed his respect for those who were in authority over him. By God's grace, he understood the interests of the people with whom he was dealing. The king wanted healthy and productive workers. The chief official wanted to keep his head. Instead of focusing exclusively on his own interests, Daniel searched for a solution that would meet their interests as well as his own. Rather than offering his personal opinions, he then suggested a way that the guard could evaluate his proposal objectively.

Test results showed that Daniel's proposed solution was valid and reasonable because he was healthier and better nourished than any of the young men who ate the royal food.

What was the final outcome?

The guard was willing to make a permanent agreement with him.

Application

Allow 20 Minutes

Negotiation does not have to be a painful tug-of-war. If approached properly, many people will respond favorably to cooperative negotiation which can allow you to find mutually beneficial solutions to common problems. Sometimes all it takes is a willingness to "look not only to your own interests, but also to the interests of others" (Philippians 2:4).

If you are presently involved in a conflict, these questions will help you to apply the principles presented in this session.

As time permits, ask for volunteers to share one or more of the questions. Also, include the prayer.

❶ Which style of negotiation is most appropriate in this situation: competitive or cooperative? Why?

❷ How can you prepare to negotiate a reasonable agreement in this situation?

❸ How can you affirm your concern and respect for your opponent?

 Facilitator's Guide: *Peacemaking*, Turning Point, P. O. Box 22127, Chattanooga, TN 37422-2127

❹ Understand interests by answering these questions:

- Which material issues need to be resolved in order to settle this conflict?

- What are your interests in this situation?

- What are your opponent's interests in this situation?

❺ What are some ways these options can be evaluated objectively and reasonably?

❻ Go on record with the Lord by writing a prayer based on the principles taught in this session.

Additional Scripture References

1 Samuel 22:6-19	*Proverbs 19:21*	*1 Corinthians 10:24*
1 Samuel 24:1-22	*Ecclesiastes 9:16*	*1 Corinthians 13:5*
Proverbs 14:8		

Closing Prayer

Ask God for wisdom as we seek to live peaceful lives before Him and with one another. Ask God for wisdom like Daniel as we confront the various challenges we each face daily.

Session 12 *Overcome Evil with Good*

"Do not be overcome by evil, but overcome evil with good" (Romans 12:21).

Introduction

Allow 10 Minutes

Opening Prayer

Invite the group to do the opening prayer. As you close the prayer time, ask the Lord to use this last session as a special time that will bring a deeper walk with Christ in the life of each group member.

Sharing Question
As a child, were you more of a troublemaker or peacemaker?

Personal response.

Self-Awareness

Allow 20–25 Minutes

Most people will respond favorably to the peacemaking principles set forth in Scripture. At times, however, you may encounter someone who simply refuses to be reconciled with you. As a result of bitterness, pride, mistrust, or greed, some people will persistently ignore repentance, reject confrontation, and resist cooperative negotiation. Sometimes a person will even continue to mistreat you deliberately.

Read Chapter 12 from *The Peacemaker* for further preparation for this session.

What are some of the natural reactions to such conduct?

To strike back or at least to stop doing good to that person.

As we have seen throughout these sessions, however, Jesus commands us to take a remarkably different course of action when we encounter such treatment: "But I tell you who hear me: Love your enemies, do good to those who hate you, bless those who curse you, pray for those who mistreat you. . . . Then your reward will be great, and you will be sons of the Most High, because he is kind to the ungrateful and wicked. Be merciful, just as you Father is merciful" (Luke 6:27-28, 35-36).

 Facilitator's Guide: *Peacemaking*, Turning Point, P. O. Box 22127, Chattanooga, TN 37422-2127

From a worldly perspective, this approach seems naive and appears to concede defeat, but the Apostle Paul knew better. He had learned that God's ways are not the world's ways. He also understood the profound power of God's principles. When he was subjected to intense and repeated personal attacks, he described his response with these words: "For though we live in the world, we do not wage war as the world does. The weapons we fight with are not the weapons of the world. On the contrary, they have divine power to demolish strongholds. We demolish arguments and every pretension that sets itself up against the knowledge of God, and we take captive every thought to make it obedient to Christ" (2 Corinthians 10:3-5).

What are some of the divine weapons to which Paul refers to in Ephesians 6:10-18 and Galatians 5:22-23?

They include scripture, prayer, truth, righteousness, the gospel, faith, love, joy, peace, patience, kindness, goodness, and self-control.

Spiritual Awareness Lead–In

To many people, these resources and qualities seem to be feeble and useless when dealing with *real* problems, yet these are the very weapons Jesus used to defeat Satan.

What weapon did Jesus use in Matthew 4:1-11 to defeat Satan?

Jesus used the Word of God. Jesus answered Satan's suggestions by saying, "It is written."

 **Spiritual-Awareness**

Allow 20–25 Minutes

Romans 12:14-21 describes how we should behave as we wield these spiritual weapons, especially when dealing with people who oppose or mistreat us:

> Bless those who persecute you; bless and do not curse. Rejoice with those who rejoice; mourn with those who mourn. Live in harmony with one another. Do not be proud, but be willing to associate with people of low position. Do not be conceited.

> Do not repay anyone evil for evil. Be careful to do what is right in the eyes of everybody. If it is possible, as far as it depends on you, live at peace with everyone. Do not take revenge, my friends, but leave room for God's wrath, for it is written: "It is mine to avenge; I will repay," says the Lord. On the contrary: "If your enemy is hungry, feed him; if he is thirsty, give him something to drink. In doing this, you will heap burning coals on his head."

> Do not be overcome by evil, but overcome evil with good.

This passage of Scripture shows that Paul understood the classic military principle that the best defense is an effective offense. He did not encourage a passive response to evil. Instead, he taught we should go on the offensive—not to beat down or destroy our opponents but to win them over, to help them see the truth, and to bring them into a right relationship with God. As this passage indicates, there are five basic principles that contribute to a victorious offensive.

Control Your Tongue

Romans 12:14
The more intense a dispute becomes, the more important it is to control your tongue.

What should be our response to those who persecute us?

> We are to bless them.

1 Peter 3:9
Even if our opponent speaks maliciously against us, we should not respond in kind.

What does Peter say about paybacks for evil and insults?

> "Do not repay evil with evil or insult with insult."

Seek Godly Advisors

Romans 12:15-16
It is difficult to battle evil alone. That is why it is important to develop relationships with people who will encourage you and give you biblically sound advice.

In light of these verses, how should we approach the good and difficult times in relationships?

> "Rejoice with those who rejoice; mourn with those who mourn. Live in harmony with one another."

Keep Doing What is Right

Romans 12:17
This verse emphasizes the importance of continuing to do what is right even when it seems that your opponent will never cooperate.

What do you think it means to "be careful to do what is right in the eyes of everybody"?

> He does not mean that we should be slaves to the opinions of others. To "be careful" means to give thought to the future, to plan in advance, or to take careful precaution. (See 2 Corinthians 8:20-21.)

Facilitator's Guide: *Peacemaking*, Turning Point, P. O. Box 22127, Chattanooga, TN 37422-2127

Recognize Your Limits

Romans 12:18
When dealing with difficult people, it is also important to recognize your limits. Even when you continue to do what is right, some people may adamantly refuse to admit you are right or to live at peace with you.

In this verse, what is the general rule for living "at peace with everyone"?

"If it is possible, as far as it depends on you, live at peace with everyone."

We should do all we can to be reconciled to others but remember that we cannot force others to do what is right. Once we have done everything within our power to resolve a conflict, we have fulfilled our responsibility to God.

Use the Ultimate Weapon

Romans 12:20-21
The final principle for responding to a stubborn opponent is described in these verses.

Describe the deliberate, focused love in these verses.

Paul's reference to "heap burning coals on his head" indicates the enormous power of deliberate, focused love. One of the most powerful weapons of his day was called "Greek fire" which was a mixture of pitch, sulphur, and burning charcoal. No soldier could resist this weapon for long. It would eventually overcome even the most determined attacker. Love has the same irresistible power.

Application

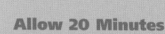

Allow 20 Minutes

The principles described in Romans 12:14-21 are applicable at every stage of a conflict, and they are echoed throughout the Bible. Applying these principles can be difficult, but it is always worth the effort because God works in and through us as we serve him as peacemakers. Paul promises: "Therefore, my dear brothers, stand firm. Let nothing move you. Always give yourselves fully to the work of the Lord, because you know that your labor in the Lord is not in vain" (1 Corinthians 15:58).

As Jesus demonstrated, the peacemaking principles set forth in Scripture provide the most effective and powerful means we could ever find to resolve conflict and restore broken relationships. He also demonstrated that peacemaking is not a passive process. Just as our Lord came to earth to purchase peace for us, we must actively and fervently pursue peace with those who oppose and mistreat us. Jesus said, "Leave your gift there in front of the altar. First go and be reconciled to your brother; then come and offer your gift" (Matthew 5:24). From this command, we can draw a simple and yet profound definition: *A peacemaker is a person who goes.*

If you are presently involved in a conflict, these questions will help you to apply the principles presented in this session.

❶ Have you been using your tongue to bless your opponents—or to speak critically of them? What will you do differently in the future in this regard?

❷ To whom can you turn for godly advice and encouragement?

❸ What can you keep on doing in this situation that is right?

❹ Have you done everything in your power to live at peace with your opponent? Is it appropriate to turn to church or civil authorities to seek assistance in resolving this dispute?

❺ Go on record with the Lord by writing a prayer based on the principles taught in this session.

Additional Scripture References		
1 Samuel 24:1-22	*Ecclesiastes 12:13*	*1 Corinthians 4:12-13*
Proverbs 20:22	*Matthew 11:28-30*	*1 Corinthians 13:4-7*
Proverbs 24:29	*Luke 6:27-28*	
Proverbs 27:5-6	*John 14:15-17*	

Closing Prayer

As time permits, ask for volunteers to share one or more of the questions. Also, include the prayer.

Thank God for His faithfulness. Thank Him for teaching us from His Word. Pray that His Word will find fruit in each life as we go out as peacemakers for Him. Thank Him for each person who participated in this group.

 Facilitator's Guide: *Peacemaking,* Turning Point, P. O. Box 22127, Chattanooga, TN 37422-2127

References

Burger, Justice Warren, "Annual Report on the State of the Judiciary," *American Bar Association Journal*, March 1982.

Elliot, Elisabeth, *Through Gates of Splendor*, Tyndale, Wheaton, 1981.

Kraybill, Ron, *Conciliation Quarterly*, Mennonite Central Committee, Summer 1987.

Lewis, C. S., *Mere Christianity*, Macmillan, New York, 1960.

Packer, J. I., *Knowing God*, InterVarsity, Downers Grove, IL, 1973.

Sande, Ken, *The Peacemaker* (second edition), Baker Book House, Grand Rapids, 1997.

Scalia, Justice Antonin, "Teaching About the Law," Quarterly 7, no. 4, Christian Legal Society, Fall 1987.

Vine, W. E., *An Expository Dictionary of Biblical Words*, Thomas Nelson, Nashville, TN, 1985.

For Further Training

If the material you have studied in this guide has excited your imagination for peacemaking, consider further training that is available from Peacemaker® Ministries. Churches sorely need many people trained in Christian conciliation. To further enhance your church or ministry's ability to guide people through conflict, you can enroll in Peacemaker Ministries Conciliator Training Program. This program is designed to equip Christians to carry out conflict counseling, mediation, and arbitration with confidence and skill. It includes a thirty-hour audio tape course and a live two-day practicum where skills are developed in realistic role plays. Individuals who desire an even higher level of competence and experience may pursue more advanced training to become a Certified Christian Conciliator™.

Trained conciliators can relieve pastors and elders from having to deal with much of the conflict that occurs in the average congregation. Many churches are also finding that this training can be used beyond their own congregation. Once they have an experienced group of conciliators available, they are able to open up their conciliation services to people in their community. These "church-based conciliation ministries" provide an excellent way to demonstrate the gospel of peace to those who are looking for assistance with their conflicts.